THE FIVE WORLDS OF OUR LIVES

Ingredients and Results of War and Revolution

A GEO-HISTORY

By The Editors of NEWSWEEK

and

The Cartographers of C. S. HAMMOND & CO., INC.

The Staff for NEWSWEEK: *Edited by* JOHN DENSON. *Art direction by* PAUL MELONE. *Photographic supervision by* TOM ORR JR. *Co-editors:* ROD GANDER, WILLIAM TUOHY, VIRGINIA KELLY, EDWIN DIAMOND. *Make-up editors:* JOHN ANDREOLA, THEODORE FRATRIK. *Editorial associates:* LUCILLE BEACHY, WALTER BENSI, JOSEPH CARTER, PHILIP C. CLARKE, ROBERT COHEN, MEL ELFIN, NANCY D. FRAZIER, DEBORAH LINK, WALTER RUNDLE, ED WERGELES, RUTH WERTHMAN. *Business manager:* S. ARTHUR DEMBNER.

The Staff for HAMMOND: MARTIN A. BACHELLER, *editor-in-chief for maps;* LIAM DUNNE and GAYLORD WELKER, *map designers;* HUGH JOHNSON, *manager, Publishers Service;* HARVEY BRITTLE, *director of production;* ERNEST J. DUPUY, ROBERT LAUGHLIN, CHARLES G. LEES JR., WALTER A. NEBIKER and ASHLEY F. TALBOT, *cartographic researchers and compilers;* EDMUND V. BALLMAN, *chief draftsman;* ARNOLD M. CARKHUFF, *art production;* BARBARA AMLICK and JEAN TILLERY, *design studies.*

NEWSWEEK, INC., MALCOLM MUIR SR., *chairman of the board and editor-in-chief;* GIBSON McCABE, *president and publisher;* JOHN DENSON, *editor;* MALCOLM MUIR JR., *executive editor;* OSBORN ELLIOTT, *managing editor;* F. E. DAVIS, CHARLES E. KANE, BORDEN R. PUTNAM, JAMES A. RICHARDS, *vice presidents;* THOMAS DARRIGAN, *treasurer.* C. S. HAMMOND & CO., INC., CALEB D. HAMMOND, *president and chairman of the board;* GEORGE M. DAVIS, *executive vice president;* STUART L. HAMMOND, *vice president and treasurer;* MARTIN A. BACHELLER, *editor-in-chief.*

Introduction to the Contents

War and revolution are born in these pages, but the seeds of soaring aspirations are here, as well. In the indestructible words of Dickens, the times were the worst and the best. The moods and modes of men changed almost as often as uncertain winters slipped into hopeful springs. Peoples and their leaders charted straight courses and crooked ones. They remade the world over and over again. Thus this volume, The Five Worlds of Our Lives, an adventure into geo-history. Its concern is not with war itself but with the world before the great wars, worlds of volcanic upheavals that led to war and changed every map, disposing of kings, tyrants and idealists with equal dispatch. This is the deadly—sometimes hopeful—shape of things man hath wrought.

The World of Imperialism

Victoria's Greater Britain—Colonialism Abroad, High Finance and New Industry at Home—The Rising Might of Germany—The Road to World War I—Resurgent France—Arts, Gaiety and Fear—The Hapsburg's Creaking Empire—Austria-Hungary Moves Toward Her Doom to the Music of the Waltz—The Romanoffs and Russia—The Court, the Cossacks and Turbulence—The Foolish Arrogance of a Power That Was Not—A Westernized Japan the Tsar Had to Reckon With—Uneasy "Peace"—The Explosion: World War I—The March Into Belgium By the Kaiser's Elite—The Warring Imperial Powers Bog Down—Revolution in Russia—The United States Enters the War—Quick Death to Tsars and Empires. **PAGES 6 TO 81.**

The World of Idealism and Upheaval

Peace and the Wilsonian Vision—The Defeated Powers—Versailles and the Vengeful—The United States and the League of Nations—The Wilson Breakdown—Adventure in Self-Determination—New Nations, New Leaders—The Break-Up of Empires—The Scandalous Harding Era in America—Anti-"Radicalism," Prohibition, Isolationism — The Coolidge Interlude — Gangland's Kingdoms—A Monkey Trial and a Flight Across the Atlantic—Hunger in Europe—The British General Strike—Hoover and the Spree in Wall Street—Black Tuesday—New and Ugly Faces at the Head of Europe's Discontented — Troubles Overwhelm America — The Great Depression—The Bonus March—The Dust Blows Over Farms—Apples for Sale. **PAGES 82 TO 121.**

The World of Dictators

Hitler and Trembling Nations—The Nazis and the Jews—Gathering Storm Clouds of World War II—The Disease of Totalitarianism Becomes a Plague—Mussolini's Italy Launches Into Modern Roman Conquest —The Failure of the League—German Soldiers On the March Again—The Fuse Ignites Civil War—Stalin, the Purger, Now the Red Master of Russia—Rattling Sabers in the Orient—Franklin D. Roosevelt and a Beginning—Recovery in Fearful Times—Munich— Hitler's Credo—Churchill Sounds the Warning—France Digs in Again at the Maginot Line—The Explosion: World War II—The Blitz—France Falls—The Deadly Surprise at Pearl Harbor—Death to Dictators—The A-Age Begins. **PAGES 122 TO 193.**

The World of Nationalism

The Great Bomb Hangs Over Mankind—The United Nations—Civil War Spreads: In China, in Greece— The Global Map Is Redrawn Again—Trials of the War Criminals—Occupation and the Debris of World War II —The Stalin Threat to Peace—The Satellites—Churchill and the "Iron Curtain"—The Marshall Plan to Stem the Red Tide—Mounting Russian Power—The Alliances: Nato, Seato, Warsaw Pact—Khrushchev Rules —Cold War; Hot War: Korea, Indo-China, Berlin—Murder of Hungary—The Middle East in Turmoil—The Communist Iron Fist in China—The Explosive Rise of the Colored Peoples—Communism Rides the Back of Nationalism—Free Africa, Churning Latin America, Threatening Asia. **PAGES 194 TO 265.**

The World of Space

The Hour of Man's Greatest Adventure—Rockets Conquer the Unknown—The Universe at the Scientist's Finger Tips—The Soaring Imaginations That Foretold Flight—The Dreamers—The Astronomers—The Mathematicians—The Rocket Pioneers—The Space Age Begins with Russia's Sputnik—The Challenge to the Free World—The Satellites Fly in Ever-Thickening Traffic — Hazards in Space Are Charted One by One — The First Living Things Return Safely from Space — The Men of the New Age, the Astronauts—The Prelude to Human Invasion of Space—The Know-How, the Machines, the Probes, the Training—The Other Side of the Moon—The Solar System—What Else to Conquer Beyond the Earth? **PAGES 266 TO 317.**

Photographic and Painting Credits Pages 318 and 319.

A global domain was hers—Victoria, as the nineteenth century gave way to the turbulent twentieth

*"The day of small nations
has passed away; the day of
Empires has come."*

Joseph Chamberlain, 1904

The World of Imperialism

Never before had there been such an empire, never would there be one quite like it again. This was Great Britain as the fateful 1900s dawned. From New Zealand to British Columbia it stretched, across Asia, Africa, and North America, the empire on which the sun never set, all ruled by the greatest lady of her age, the tiny, frumpy, literal-minded, implacably courageous Empress, Queen Victoria.

The nineteenth century was the age of the modern empire, and the nineteenth century had belonged to England. From London, her conquerors, her administrators, her Tommies in spit-and-polish legions went out to take about a third of Africa—the Gold Coast, Somaliland, Nigeria, Kenya, the Anglo-Egyptian Sudan, British South Africa—and to incorporate all of India and Burma, the Straits Settlements, British New Guinea.

The British Empire almost doubled in size and population in this century; its wealth increased almost beyond measure. Now it had the fabled wealth of the Indies: Tea, cotton, rubber, mica, petroleum. It had the wealth of Africa: Diamonds and cotton, tobacco, asbestos, tin and zinc. At home, Britain had energy, industrial and financial skill.

Victoria's navies controlled the oceans of the world, from Halifax to Hong Kong—Britannia, indeed, ruled the waves. But Britain had been challenged—and Britain was deep in another war, fighting the Boers in South Africa. It may be a measure of Britain's power that, when Queen Victoria was informed of the first British reverses in that savage little war, she answered: "We are not interested in the possibilities of defeat. They do not exist."

So Victoria spoke, as she had for 63 years of empire building, and the grand design of the Victorian Age became a part of the twentieth century.

Abroad, *Queen Victoria had long fared well. Aladdin (Disraeli) hands her the crown of India*

The Victorian Age had an opulence no English ruler had dared dream of. What other Western queen wore the crown of far-off India? But for all its grandeur, it was at the same time an English world curiously insular and self-contained, in which cartoonists could take private jibes at Victoria's cold displeasure at the youthful hi-jinks of her eldest son—one day to be the ruler of all she had created—Edward VII. Though their empire stretched everywhere, most Englishmen at home had a business-only concern with anything beyond the English Channel. The far reaches of the empire—in India, in Africa—were not separate countries, but simply outposts of the empire, mysterious dark lands where Englishmen went to rule, and to fight. Victoria's England was a calm and comfortable world, where elegantly-clad ladies and gentlemen promenaded in Hyde Park, and there seemed no end to the flow of riches from the colonies, nor to the supply of Englishmen to fight for them. The great houses glowed with the lights of mannerly dinner parties, silver at its brightest, linen whiter than white.

Holidaying *in the Highlands, the Queen found contentment*

In the palace, *a mother's trouble. An angry Victoria punishes the playboy Edward VII, Prince of Wales*

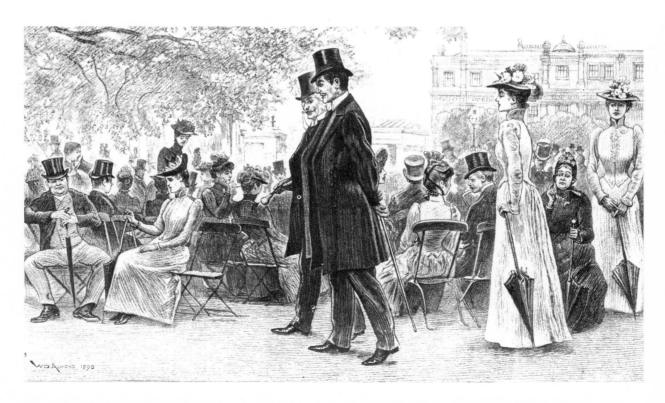

Victorian *ladies and gentlemen enjoy a leisurely outing in London's fashionable Hyde Park*

9

The empire had not been easy in the making. There had been the vigor and audaciousness of the most trusted of Victoria's statesmen—Benjamin Disraeli. With the great William Gladstone, Disraeli alternated in the post of Prime Minister for a full generation—a generation that saw the greatest strides in securing a domain for Victoria. Disraeli, the Conservative, and Gladstone, the Liberal, differed on means and methods, but not in their devotion. These two statesmen saw to it that Her Majesty's far-flung viceroys and colonial governors, ministers and consuls, strengthened Britain's position in India, Afghanistan, Persia, Kenya, Nigeria, the Sudan, and Egypt. And it was a diplomatic master-stroke—Disraeli's buying the bankrupt Khedive of Egypt's shares in the French-built Suez Canal—that won for England the crucial link between Europe, Africa and the Far East.

Benjamin Disraeli, *the architect of empire*

A Royal Dragoon *in South Africa, far from home*

The empire won, *the Battle of Omdurman ends Sudanese resistance*

Rhodes *(left) was accused of Napoleonic tactics in carving African empire*

Victoria's statesmen's triumphs in Parliament could be no greater than the bravery of Englishmen in the field. In distant places of the world, in jungles and in deserts, the British soldier fought and the adventurous pioneered. It took a special breed of man—like Field Marshal Kitchener, "Chinese" Gordon, and Cecil Rhodes, South African empire builder. Lampooned as a "Napoleon" by critics, Rhodes nevertheless stretched British rule to the land that bears his name—Rhodesia. From the distant places came back stories of victories and massacres, of glory and death. The names of the battles still live: Khartoum, Omdurman, and Lucknow. All through British history the names of such battles were woven into poetry and drama, novel and picture, a part of the empire that will endure forever.

Briesemeister Elliptical Equal-Area Projection of the World. Courtesy of The American Geographical Society.

British America
3,700,000 Square Miles

Victorian Britain—To the Far Ends

There was not a continent in the world, at the height of Victoria's reign,
but that part of it was England. Almost half of North America was part
of that empire, and slices of Central and of South America; a vast part of
Africa; a whole continent in Australia; some of the richest lands of Asia—
all this supplemented with tiny islands and holdings around the globe that

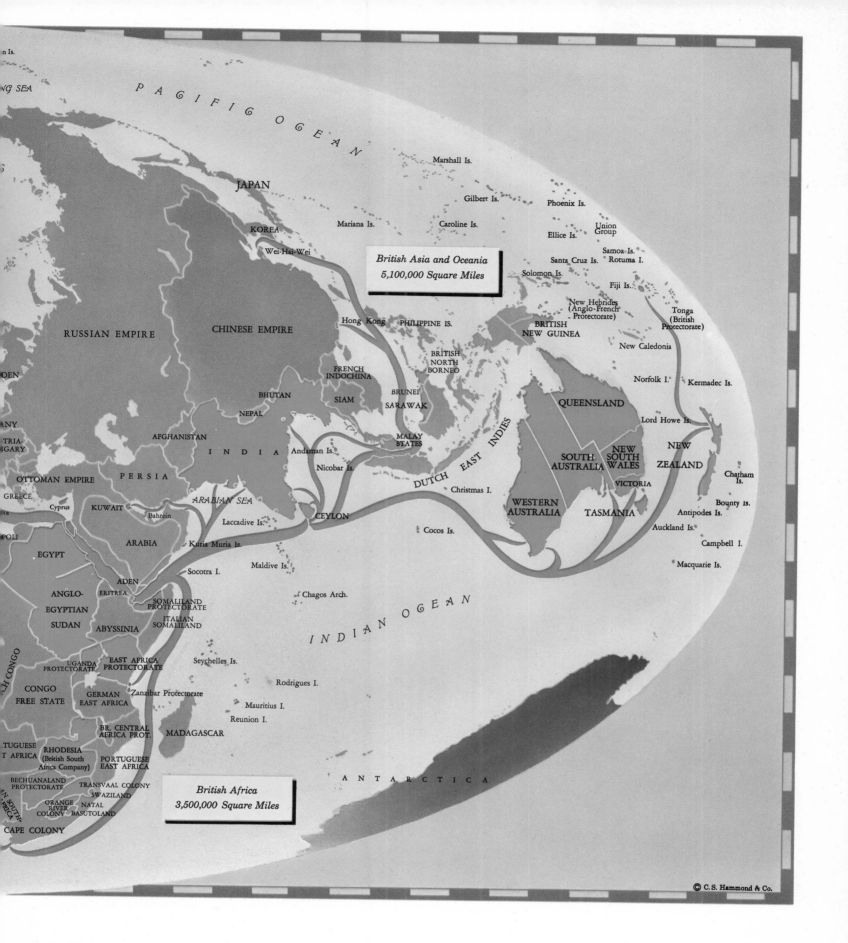

British Asia and Oceania
5,100,000 Square Miles

British Africa
3,500,000 Square Miles

© C.S. Hammond & Co.

had accrued to Britain through her centuries of exploring, colonizing, conquering new lands since the days when England's great earlier woman sovereign, Elizabeth I, had sent her galleons coursing the oceans of the world. As in the days of Elizabeth, it was British seapower that enabled Britain to expand and maintain her empire. Plying sealanes which circled the globe (marked in red on the map), the largest naval and merchant fleet the world had ever known transported the rich cargoes which made Britain the greatest of all trading nations.

13

For the British colonist (here in India), there was a life of ease in Victoria's lands

3 million Sudanese

A quarter million Malays

220 million Indians

A quarter million Chines

For the British colonist's wife, *all the luxuries home rarely offered*

For Englishmen living in the far distant reaches of the empire—once the fighting was done—there were compensations and power. Englishmen ruled peoples of all hues—the yellow, the brown, the black shown on these pages. The "white man's burden" came to be worth it: Creature comforts far beyond the comforts of home, servants galore, and the warming southern sun. To Africa and Asia, the British brought the uplifting benefits of civilization; in some cases, though, the benefits proved to be merely the exploitation of native labor. And, curiously, imperialism contained the elements of its own destruction: The spark of advancement produced the fires of nationalism that would one day consume the whole colonial structure.

30 million Africans

7 million Burmese

A half million Arabians

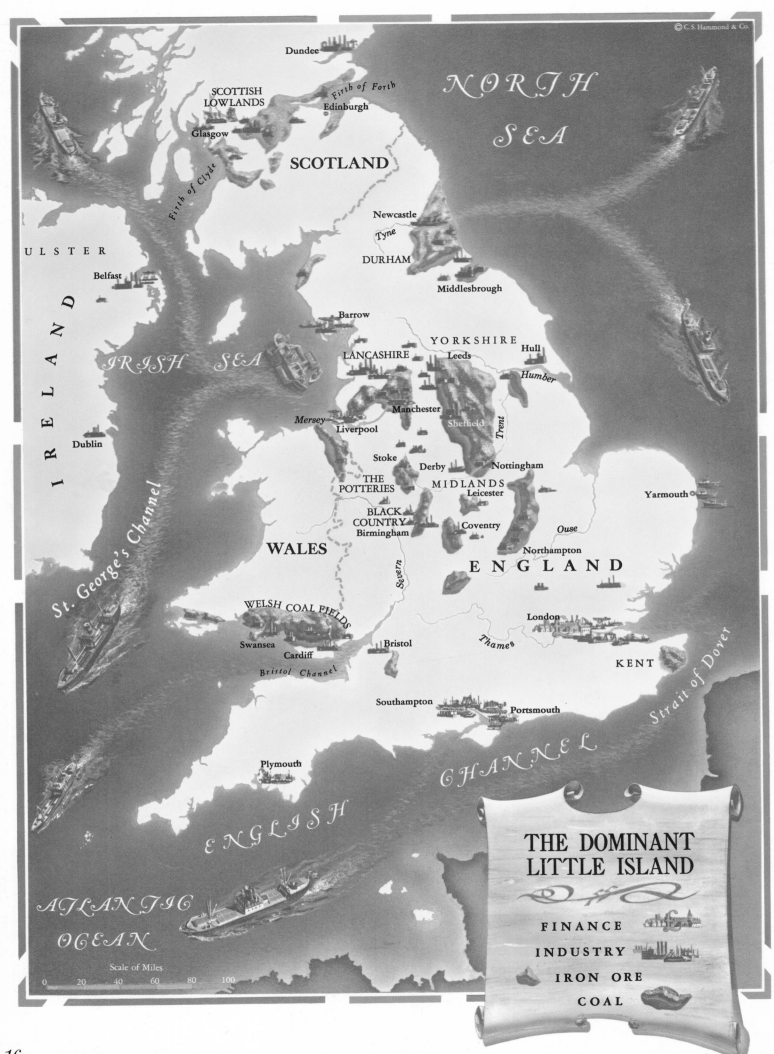

NORTH SEA

SCOTLAND

IRELAND

ULSTER

IRISH SEA

St. George's Channel

ATLANTIC OCEAN

ENGLISH CHANNEL

WALES

ENGLAND

Dundee

SCOTTISH LOWLANDS

Edinburgh

Firth of Forth

Glasgow

Firth of Clyde

Newcastle

Tyne

DURHAM

Middlesbrough

Belfast

Barrow

YORKSHIRE

LANCASHIRE

Leeds

Hull

Humber

Dublin

Mersey

Manchester

Sheffield

Trent

Liverpool

Stoke

Derby

Nottingham

THE POTTERIES

MIDLANDS

Leicester

Yarmouth

BLACK COUNTRY

Birmingham

Coventry

Ouse

Northampton

Severn

Bristol

London

Thames

KENT

WELSH COAL FIELDS

Swansea

Cardiff

Bristol Channel

Southampton

Portsmouth

Strait of Dover

Plymouth

Scale of Miles

0 20 40 60 80 100

© C. S. Hammond & Co.

THE DOMINANT LITTLE ISLAND

FINANCE

INDUSTRY

IRON ORE

COAL

Britain at Home

All through the nineteenth century a vast change had been taking place, a change that would prove a more solid under-pinning for a long-lasting Britain than colonies beyond the Atlantic island. This change was an upheaval that has been called the greatest of them all—the Industrial Revolution. It was an uncanny historic coincidence, the development of an industrial empire at just the moment rich raw materials of the empire were ready to be exploited. Now England was the most powerful investor on earth. In the coal pits of England and Wales, men, women and children worked to mine the fuel for the mills and factories. But by the end of Victoria's reign, too, there had been a social revolution that freed the women and children, and England emerged as the financial, industrial and geographic giant, launching into a new century without a visible blemish on the horizon.

Through the Bank of England, *the blood of finance flowed through the heart of empire expansion abroad, industrial revolution at home*

Joined with British finance was British coal that stoked the Industrial Revolution

Lloyd's of London insured the great commercial fleet

Victoria was dead at 81, and the empire mourned. But as her great merchant fleet gathered up the riches of empire, and the Lutine Bell at Lloyd's tolled the glad news of storm-struck ships found safe, the sad news of an occasional ship lost, Britain continued to thrive. Edward VII, the naughty prince of Victoria's earlier years, was crowned in Westminster Abbey, to reign nine short years; and even the clothes worn by fashionable ladies and gentlemen were changing—from the staid to the dashing. But while dandies might strut in Bond Street, at Whitehall—and around the world—British diplomacy was at work, ever-strengthening the outposts and lifelines, ever-promoting alliances to insure their safety. The scramble for raw materials and strategic position in Africa, Asia, and the Pacific were bringing the great colonial powers—England, France, Russia, and Germany—close to jarring collision. For a time, friction between Britain and France over lush prizes in Egypt threatened to bring these lordly, traditional enemies into violent conflict. But suave diplomats amicably resolved the dispute, and adept statesmanship turned the bitter Anglo-French rivalry into a firm alliance—much to the surprise, and dismay, of Imperial Germany.

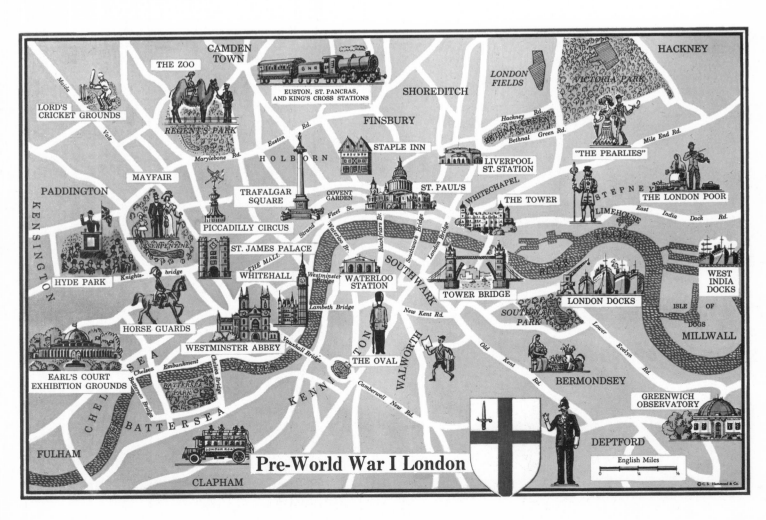

Pre-World War I London

In pomp and circumstance *at Westminster Abbey, Edward VII is crowned ruler of the empire*

Edwardian lady, *frills and feathers*

Edwardian gentleman, *top hat and cane*

At Edward's death, George V, quiet and reserved, ascended the British throne. Though few were aware of it in 1910, the next few years were to change the stream of history. By means of her alliances with France and Russia, England was closing a ring around Germany—partly through fear of German militarism, partly to protect economic interests. For support, Germany turned to Austria, and both were willing to flex their muscles. Thus, massive hostile forces were inexorably set in motion. The halcyon days were over. Britain faced the bloodiest test of her existence. The might of England would diminish in the mud of Flanders fields. George V would see all this, but he would not live to see even the faint beginnings of the dissolution of Victoria's empire, nor the second great war which would rain destruction on England herself. The Germans would come again and again in flaming chariots of death.

For George V, *four years of rule before the holocaust*

The elite Grenadier Guards *who symbolized proud service to the Crown would face their test in France*

The first Kaiser, Wilhelm I, creator of the most powerful army in the world

Imperial Germany's Thrust Outward

The Holy Roman Empire—in what respect is it holy, or Roman, or an empire? With such a sardonic question, Voltaire characterized the impotent conglomeration of petty princes, ecclesiastical states, and free cities which for a thousand years held uncertain sway over the Germans of Central Europe. Germany was little more than a pawn in the wars of the pre-1800s, lacking unity, a prey to invasion from both East and West.

But in Prussia, where the Hohenzollern king had the allegiance of the finest of professional soldiers, the proud Junkers, the weapon had slowly been forged to make the Germans a united people and the most powerful in all of Europe.

Gneisenau, Scharnhorst, Clausewitz—these were the generals who revolutionized military tactics by conceiving the idea of a permanent General Staff, that cold, efficient planning arm which soon gave the Prussian army the advantage over its European rivals. The Prussians would strike out before the turning of the century; they would subdue the French and move relentlessly onward to worse and bloodier wars. The emerging German Empire was being forged into a sword of steel.

The Iron Chancellor, *Count Otto von Bismarck, molded modern, military Germany*

Prussian generals *produced such mobile, disciplined, maneuvering armies (shown here prepared to attack in columns by company) that they seemed nearly invincible*

W hen the soldierly Wilhelm I came to power, he faced immediate crisis. Demanding an increase in the size of the army, he was opposed by Parliament which refused to levy the necessary funds. In 1862, prepared to abdicate, Wilhelm I turned to Otto von Bismarck as the last hope for maintaining Junker supremacy.

The trust was well placed. The new Prime Minister, the most skilled diplomat of his age, became the symbol of Prussian greatness. In ten short years, Bismarck redrew the map of Central Europe and created modern Germany. This was the Germany the world would be forced to reckon with for nearly 100 years after Wilhelm I's crisis with his Parliament.

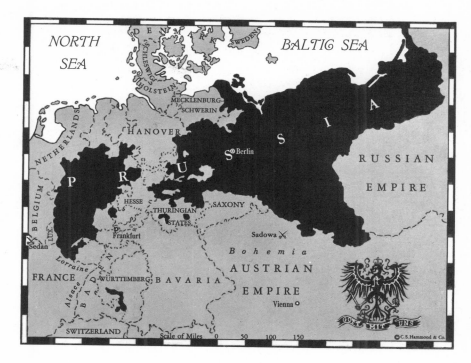

Germany, as it was divided before Bismarck, an anachronistic holdover from the Holy Roman Empire

Germany, after it was united at last by Bismarck's guile and Prussian steel

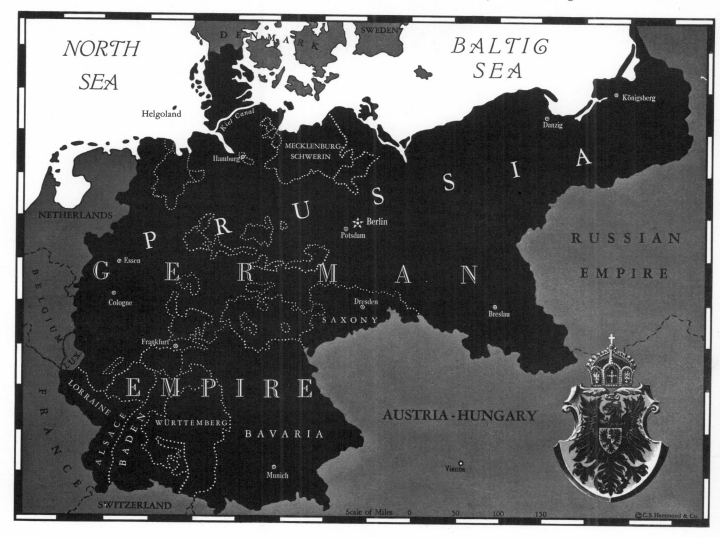

The Iron and the Blood

Bismarck had said it: "The great questions of the time will be decided by blood and iron." And Europe did not wait long to see such nineteenth century "wisdom" put to the test. Under the brilliant Gen. Helmuth von Moltke, the army of iron was ready. First the proud House of Hapsburg was dealt with. Warrior-Prussians smashed the Austrians at Sadowa, and the northern German states came under Prussian domination.

In 1870 came a greater test for a "greater Germany." Bismarck maneuvered France into declaring war. Still using the antiquated tactic of direct frontal attack, the over-confident French were encircled by Moltke at Sedan. In the face of this disaster Léon Gambetta swiftly raised a re-

placement army, but could not prevent the fall of Paris. In a burst of nationalistic enthusiasm, the south German states joined the north. With his troops, Wilhelm I crossed a battered, defeated France (this is a painting of the war's ravages) to the great palace of Versailles. There, in the Hall of Mirrors, Wilhelm I was crowned first Emperor of a unified Germany.

With this stroke of iron, Bismarck cried that he was a man of peace. The new Germany was satiated, so he told Europe. She needed time to consolidate her gains, to build her economy. By devising an intricate network of alliances, Bismarck did keep the peace, but it was an uneasy peace and one only such a skilled, self-serving statesman as he could control. Under Wilhelm I, Bismarck was virtually a dictator, but in 1888, the old Emperor died. Wilhelm II gained the crown. Germany had not forgotten what the Prussians had taught her. She had learned to like the goose step.

Wilhelm II, *arrogant grandson of the first Kaiser, made bombastic speeches and paraded his grandiose ambitions for a greater Germany*

The boastful Kaiser's favorite pastime—reviewing the elite of his legions

Violence was honor for young Germans, a saber slash in the dueling pit was a hero's scar

"There is only one master in this country, and I am he."

Vain, impulsive Kaiser Wilhelm II, whose self-confidence was near-pathological, worshipped the art of war. He had a childlike love of military parades and maneuvers; he would in effect be his own Prime Minister, his own chief of the General Staff. Within two years he forced Bismarck's resignation, and, with the cry, a "place in the sun," brought the new German imperialism to a destructive peak.

Bismarck had fanned the flames of German nationalism, but for a different purpose. The old Chancellor had cannily manipulated the appeal of pan-Germanism to unite all the Teutonic factions—landowning Junkers with Ruhr industrialists, Protestant north with Catholic south, Socialists with Conservatives. But Wilhelm II's political maneuvers were the ingredients for war.

Germany gloried in her new-found strength, her army was the most powerful in the world. She was mainland Europe's greatest economic power, rivaling England—Stinnes, Krupp, Thyssen created baronies of coal and steel, while Wilhelm II rattled his saber—and, it seemed, no political force was great enough to stop him.

The nation which produced Nietzsche and his concept of the superman, was now envisioned as the super state. Gone was the Bismarckian web of alliance in favor of the "free hand." Germany would go it alone and with a vengeance.

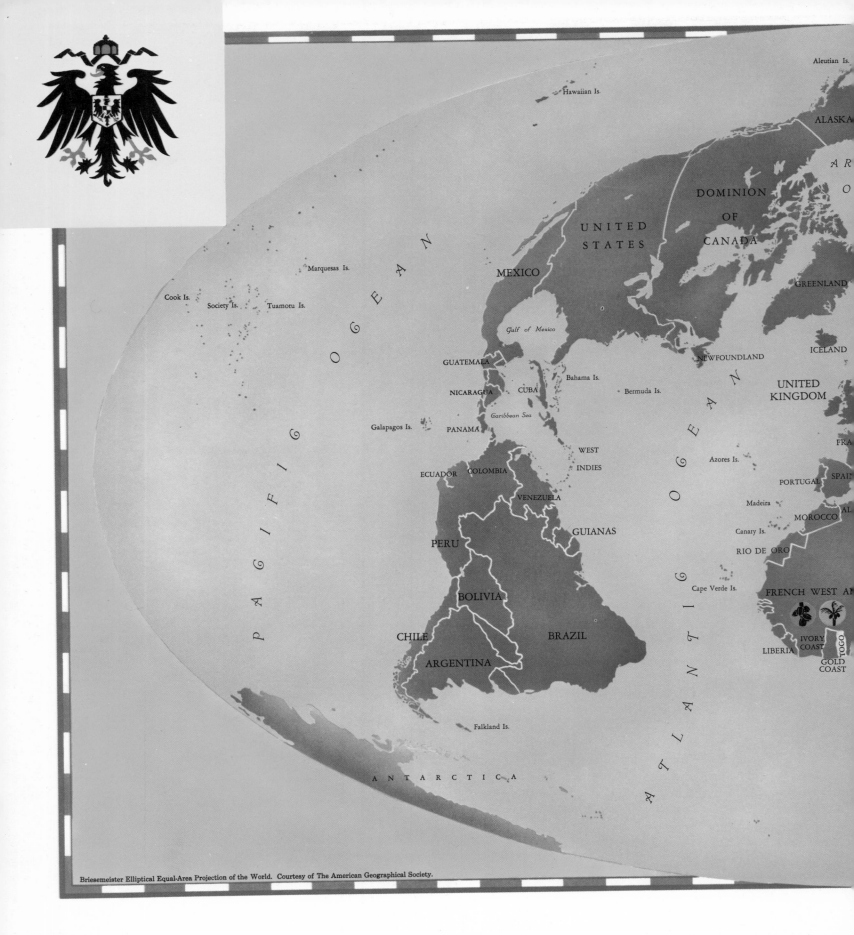

Briesemeister Elliptical Equal-Area Projection of the World. Courtesy of The American Geographical Society.

The German Empire's Long Reach

Late as a nation, Germany was handicapped in the race for overseas colonies, yet by World War I, the Black Eagle was raised over 1,232,127 square miles of territory in Africa and the Pacific.

Ironically, Bismarck, who directed most of this expansion, was in spirit opposed to it. Faced with a rising clamor to support German interests in

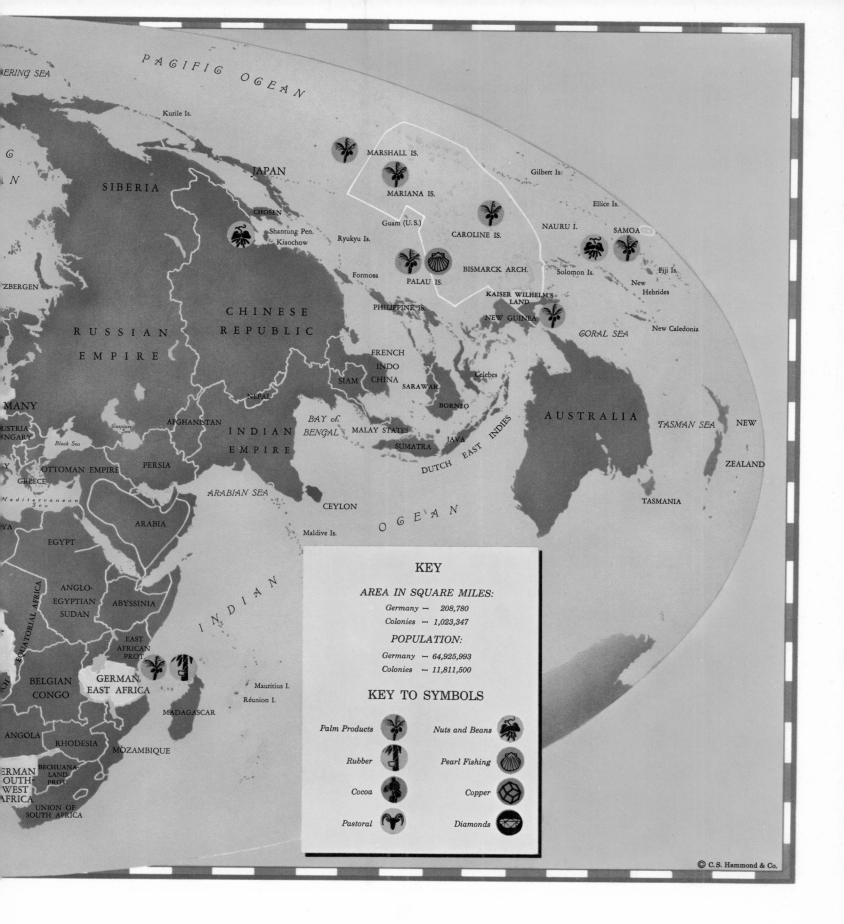

PACIFIC OCEAN

BERING SEA

Kurile Is.

JAPAN

SIBERIA

CHOSEN

Shantung Pen.
Kiaochow

MARSHALL IS.

MARIANA IS.

Gilbert Is.

Ellice Is.

RUSSIAN
EMPIRE

CHINESE
REPUBLIC

Ryukyu Is.

Guam (U.S.)

CAROLINE IS.

NAURU I.

SAMOA

Formosa

PALAU IS.

BISMARCK ARCH.

Solomon Is.

Fiji Is.

New
Hebrides

MANY

AFGHANISTAN

Caspian
Sea

FRENCH
INDO
CHINA

SIAM

NEPAL

PHILIPPINE IS.

KAISER WILHELM'S
LAND

NEW GUINEA

CORAL SEA

New Caledonia

AUSTRIA
HUNGARY

Black Sea

PERSIA

INDIAN
EMPIRE

BAY of
BENGAL

MALAY STATES

SARAWAK

BORNEO

Celebes

TASMAN SEA

NEW

Y

OTTOMAN EMPIRE

GREECE

Mediterranean
Sea

ARABIA

ARABIAN SEA

SUMATRA

JAVA

DUTCH EAST INDIES

ZEALAND

YA

EGYPT

CEYLON

Maldive Is.

OCEAN

TASMANIA

INDIAN

ANGLO-
EGYPTIAN
SUDAN

ABYSSINIA

Mauritius I.

Réunion I.

KEY

AREA IN SQUARE MILES:

Germany — 208,780
Colonies — 1,023,347

POPULATION:

Germany — 64,925,993
Colonies — 11,811,500

KEY TO SYMBOLS

BELGIAN
CONGO

EAST
AFRICAN
PROT.

GERMAN
EAST AFRICA

MADAGASCAR

ANGOLA

RHODESIA

MOZAMBIQUE

ERMAN
OUTH-
WEST
FRICA

BECHUANA-
LAND
PROT.

UNION OF
SOUTH AFRICA

Palm Products	Nuts and Beans
Rubber	Pearl Fishing
Cocoa	Copper
Pastoral	Diamonds

© C.S. Hammond & Co.

Southeast Europe, a course he was sure would lead to war, the old Chancellor used the colonies to slake the Germans' thirst for territory.

Wilhelm II had no such lofty motive. Germany would prove she was the greatest world power. A huge naval shipbuilding program was launched to defy British supremacy on the sea. Then, flying in the face of France, the Kaiser gave support to Moroccan independence. But he succeeded only in uniting those two long-time enemies, France and England. As Germany pressed her claim to an overseas empire, the march to war was unstoppable. There was no turning back. The European powers armed to the teeth.

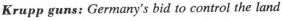
The submarine: Germany's bid to control the seas

cross the channel, Britain watched Germany's greatly-expanding arsenal with the nagging fear that such deadly stores could only mean war. Why else would the Kaiser be building his navy?

It is doubtful that Wilhelm himself could have answered that question. Notorious for playing favorites, he now had lent his ear to Navy Secretary Alfred von Tirpitz. The Navy program was strongly supported by the Ruhr industrialists fattening on the purchase of steel. And for Berlin in the 1900s—and for Berliners strolling in the Tiergarten, boating on the Spree, and sipping apéritifs in Kurfürstendamm cafés—there was a simple answer: A great nation should have a great navy, and Germany was the greatest of nations.

Krupp guns: Germany's bid to control the land

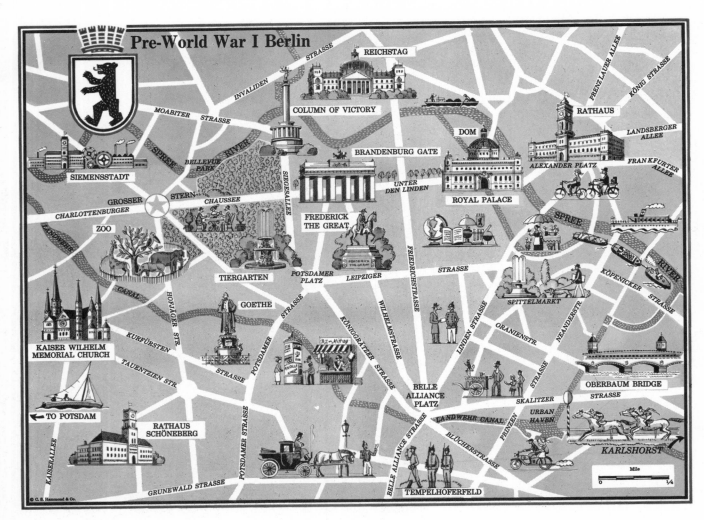

Pre-World War I Berlin

Resurgent France

Lights blazed again in Paris. The humiliation and hurt which the Prussians had brought to France began to heal as the nineteenth century faded. (Only the loss of beloved Alsace-Lorraine plagued France.) Frenchmen listened to jack boots pounding the cobblestones of Germany, the sounds—as sure as dawn—of another, greater war. France was watchful, but the sounds in Paris were never gayer. Colonialism spread and bred new riches. Frenchmen argued the old arguments—republic or monarchy? And, for a time, a new King—or an Emperor for a new France and her colonies—seemed a real possibility. But the kingmakers, though they plotted as only French politicians can, finally failed. France was rising again; her arts flowered; her commerce flourished. Statesmen and generals danced to rollicking music, but they knew, as millions of other Frenchmen knew, that a modern army was thundering a chorus of marching songs across the Rhine.

Marshal MacMahon, *President of the French Republic, favored a monarchy*

Léon Gambetta *foiled MacMahon's royalist schemes*

Jules Ferry *was the architect of French colonialism*

The Dance at Bougival *by Pierre Auguste Renoir*

Surely the gaiety of France was frenetic, the inevitable reaction to the oppressiveness of Paris under Prussian siege during the War of 1870, when the rodents of Paris were pounced upon for meat. But the cultural revival was real and earnest. There were new writers—the great Emile Zola and Anatole France, Paul Verlaine and Guy de Maupassant. They crusaded, they entertained and they helped restore French pride. There were the new artists—Monet, Manet, Renoir, Degas. They put their times on canvas but they did more. With them came the first adventures into impressionism. The arts were lively, indeed. Paris had a champagne air and male eyes glistened when pretty Parisiennes danced the daring can-can.

Jane Avril *at the Moulin Rouge by Toulouse-Lautrec*

Promenading Parisians *on the Boulevard des Italiens by Pissarro*

And society *going to the theater in Renoir's 'The Loge'*

Now Paris, late in the nineteenth century, was taking on the look that was to be her image to the world even until today: Paris the gay, Paris the delightful, Paris the city of light. Now British and Americans—visitors from all over the world—began to throng Paris, and boulevards were always crowded with foreigners fallen in love with the city, with top-hatted elite and beret-covered Bohemians. Only determined politicians mourned the Second Empire which the War of 1870 ended. The royal aristocrat vanished when the Empress Eugénie fled to England. Under the new Republic, the aristocracy was of a different kind—an aristocracy of wealth won from the colonies and a reviving Republic. There were only polite bows to the old aristocracy whose court was no more.

Expositions were a delight to Frenchmen. Brightest and biggest in the generation before the first world war was the Paris Exposition of 1889. Tourists were charmed by the dancing girls, and the baroque exhibition halls celebrated for their ornate interplay of light and gushing water. But the greatest attraction of all was a wondrous new structure which forever after would be the city's most famous landmark. This was the Eiffel Tower, created by the engineer Gustave Eiffel. The tower not only dominated the Paris skyline—984 feet high, the tallest structure in the world—it also dominated the columns of the newspapers and dinner-table conversations for a decade. A monstrosity, a gargoyle, an abomination, it was called, the structure now as much a symbol of Paris as the meandering Seine and bridges made of stone for arm-in-arm strollers to walk on.

As Paris boomed into the new century, the Eiffel Tower rose over the city

The lower structure, *the tower took two years to build*

The ornate Electricity Building *helped attract 39 million people to the 1900 exposition*

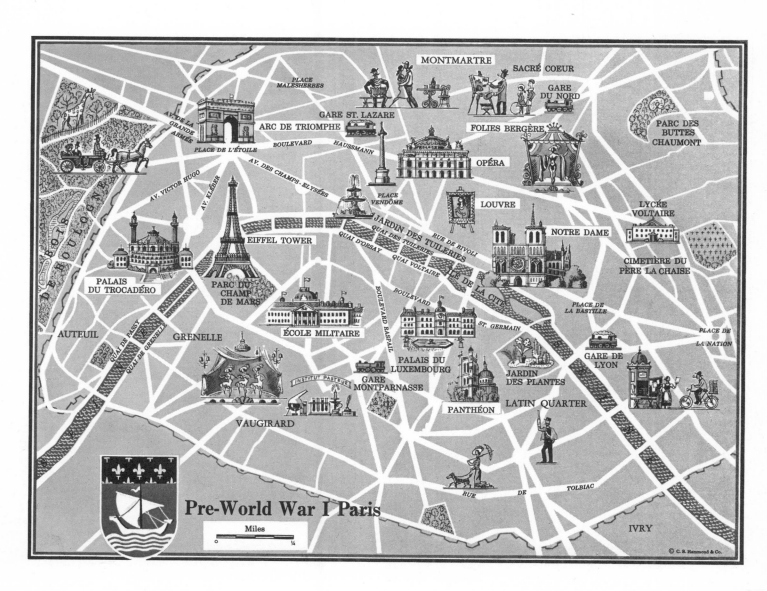

Pre-World War I Paris

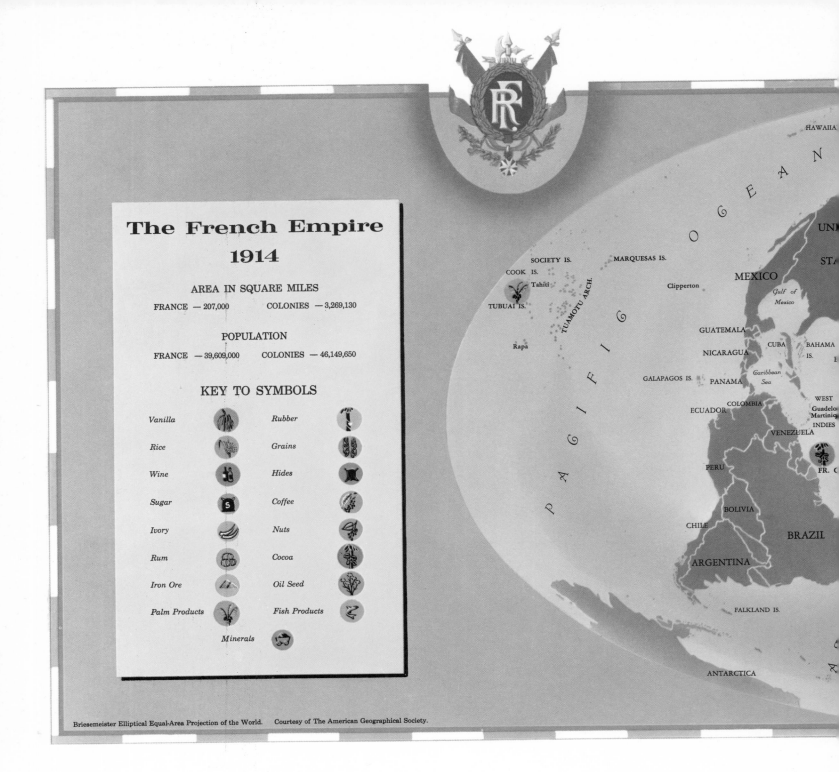

The French Empire
1914

AREA IN SQUARE MILES

FRANCE — 207,000   COLONIES — 3,269,130

POPULATION

FRANCE — 39,609,000   COLONIES — 46,149,650

KEY TO SYMBOLS

Vanilla		Rubber	
Rice		Grains	
Wine		Hides	
Sugar		Coffee	
Ivory		Nuts	
Rum		Cocoa	
Iron Ore		Oil Seed	
Palm Products		Fish Products	
	Minerals		

Briesemeister Elliptical Equal-Area Projection of the World.   Courtesy of The American Geographical Society.

The French met fierce resistance at the Battle of Mouzaïa in conquest of Algeria

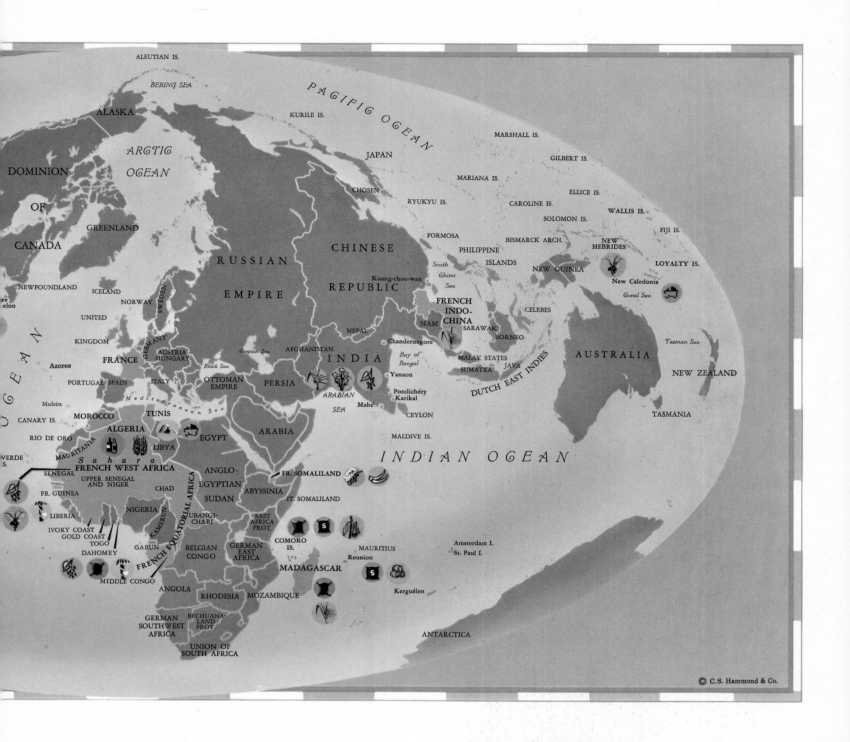

A Global Domain Welded to Paris

France was far, far behind England in the race for a modern empire: France had not fully understood the need for empire that drove Britain to one conquest after another. The nineteenth century was more than three-quarters done before France, too, reached out for possessions abroad. And France had one more motive for empire than the others. Like England and Germany, empire was a matter of historic prestige for a first-rate world power; and like them, as an emerging industrial power, France needed colonies to supply her factories with raw materials. But France also, at this time of history, needed above all else new conquests to restore the damage to her

national pride and to her European boundaries in losing the War of 1870. It was in 1881 that France began to drive eastward from Algeria into Tunisia. Within a few years in Southeast Asia she conquered Annam and Tonkin; she prepared for the conquest of the Sudan, the Congo, and Madagascar; she occupied oases of the Sahara with the famous French Foreign Legion; she moved into Morocco. In the end—just prior to World War I—France was second only to Britain as the world's greatest colonial power; and the chief executor of her colonial policy, Louis Lyautey, spoke grandly, if inaccurately, of a France of a hundred million inhabitants.

France had felt the full force of the Prussian-German drive to dominate the Continent, and no sooner had the consequences of the War of 1870 emerged than Frenchmen of vision realized that another Franco-German war would come. In the years that closed the nineteenth century and opened the twentieth, France grew stronger. The mills and the foundries of her expanding industrial system began to develop the muscle that could defend the nation in war. Her armies were no longer the tattered legions that had fallen before Prussian might. Every Frenchman feared he would have to fight, but he danced into the night and hoped to hold back the day. Ahead lay the final tragedy in which no victor emerges except tragedy itself. Despite the forges that flared through the nights and despite the valor of her greatest armies—despite even the fact that she was one of the victors— France did not and could not win the war that was to come. By the hundreds of thousands, Frenchmen were to die. It was the first of the wars that had no victors, only the vanquished. No one knew it but the War of 1870 had been the last of the "genteel wars," as a cynic once observed.

Around the clock, *foundries gave France muscle for the conflict that lay ahead*

A proud army emerged quickly from the Franco-Prussian debacle

On the eve of World War I, *French infantry officer (left) and foot soldiers*

All Was Hapsburg

Like a fluffy, frosty, pink Viennese pastry, the Austro-Hungarian Empire that stood astride the map of Central Europe at the turn of the century was, beneath an impressive façade, little more than an empty shell. Although she stretched from the Tyrolean Alps to the Ukrainian steppes, Austria-Hungary was a historical accident, a bizarre collection of geographical odds and ends strung together with the loosest of political and economic ties. Divided in language, culture, temperament, and national aspirations, the Germans, Magyars, Italians, and myriad Slavs who populated this polyglot state had but one unifying symbol—Emperor Franz Josef, last of the great Hapsburg kings. Austria fought two wars in the twentieth century but, measured by reality, she never really emerged from the nineteenth century.

The Emperor, a Spartan in his habits, authoritarian in his manners, archly conservative in his politics, struggled manfully for almost 70 years to hold his brittle empire together, to make it something more than a private estate. But all through his long reign, while his great capital of Vienna danced and laughed as though every day would be the last, Franz Josef was beset and bewildered. Pressures and problems swirled within and around Austria-Hungary. From the north and south came the irresistible surge of new-born German and Italian nationalism. On the east, the Russian Tsars fused the Balkan tinder box with anti-Austrian intrigue. Internally, the Czechs, the Slovaks, Serbs, etc., schemed for independence. Here a genius of statecraft might have created a solid state. But the Emperor was no genius. So, almost from the day he ascended the throne in 1848, Franz Josef was doomed. The twentieth century would make the failure one of crushing disaster.

Waltzers around Emperor Franz Josef at a lavish court ball at the Imperial Palace

In royal procession, *Franz Josef departs for high mass in his sumptuous coach*

The ornate stairway *in the Belvedere Palace, built for military hero, Prince Eugen*

The Austrian Army's *regal bearing, elegant uniforms, splendid mustaches*

The Vienna coffee house *where papers headlined approach of doom*

There was no place in the world quite like Vienna at the time of the Hapsburg Empire. For pomp, pageantry and the stately dignity of royal processions, it was the equal of London. In culture, intellect and spirited night life, it rivaled Paris. And as the capital of Franz Josef's hybrid monarchy, it was as cosmopolitan as New York.

Yet, for all the qualities it had in common with other cities, imperial Vienna was unique. Perhaps it was the baroque splendor of its public buildings, the relaxed amiability of its coffee houses, or even the dashing glamor of its soldiers (who were usually more adept on the dance floor than on the battlefield). Actually, what gave the stately Hapsburg capital its intoxicating élan was the distinctive charm of the Viennese themselves, compounded as it was of nonchalance, gay good spirits, sentiment and a curiously light-hearted melancholy.

43

At the Spanish Riding Academy in Vienna, the equestrian art achieved grandeur

From the far reaches of the empire, the talented, the scholarly, the aspiring converged on Vienna, lured by its regal cultural traditions, its superb museums, its renowned university, its great medical school, its flourishing theater and its respect for the life of the mind. Here, a Jewish doctor from Moravia named Sigmund Freud brewed the potion called psychoanalysis. Here, a Hungarian journalist named Theodor Herzl first propagated the doctrines of Zionism. And here, too, a struggling, provincial, art student named Adolf Hitler began nurturing his monstrous grudge against mankind.

The golden jubilee concert of the Vienna Philharmonic in 1910

As Paris was the city of light, so music made Vienna the city of sound. It bubbled up everywhere—in the ornate opera house, in the great concert hall, in the Prater amusement park, in the wine gardens of Grinzing, in the restaurants and rathskellers, and in the ancient streets themselves. Vienna, once the home of Haydn, Mozart, Schubert, and Beethoven, under Franz Josef now sheltered a new generation of musical genius—Anton Bruckner, Gustav Mahler, Richard Strauss, Franz Lehár, and the most Viennese of them all, Johann Strauss, waltz-maker to the world.

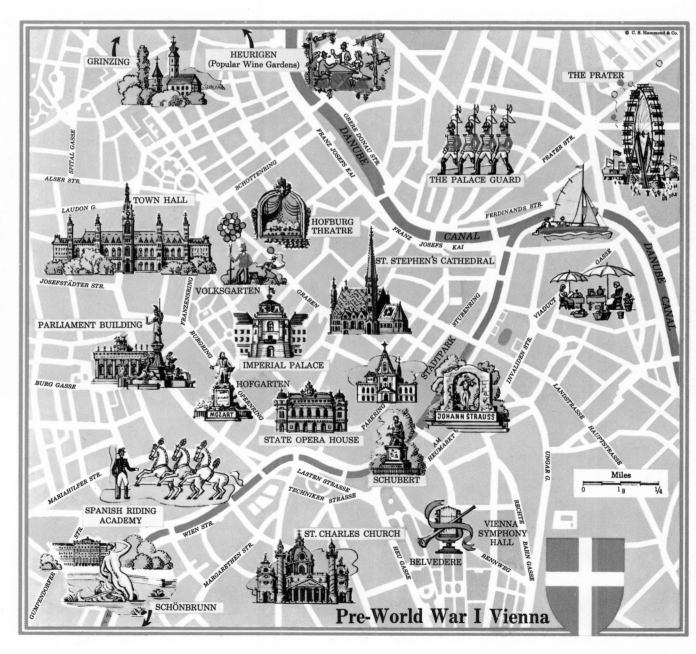

Pre-World War I Vienna

Grandeur in death, *the tomb of Empress Maria Theresa of Hapsburg*

After escaping assassination, *the Emperor walks among the people*

Although a mere vestigial relic of the once powerful Holy Roman Empire, Austria-Hungary was forever linked to its heroic past by those eternal institutions—the Hapsburgs and the Roman Catholic Church. (Magnificent St. Stephen's—opposite page—was the heart of Austrian Catholicism.) In almost 700 years of rule, the Hapsburgs had not only produced notable and pious sovereigns like Empress Maria Theresa, but had twice stemmed the Moslem tide in Europe. As heir to this tradition, Franz Josef was a vigorous defender of the faith; and, after he narrowly escaped an assassin's knife in Vienna in 1853, the Emperor became an even more loyal son of the Church, giving it new power and privilege.

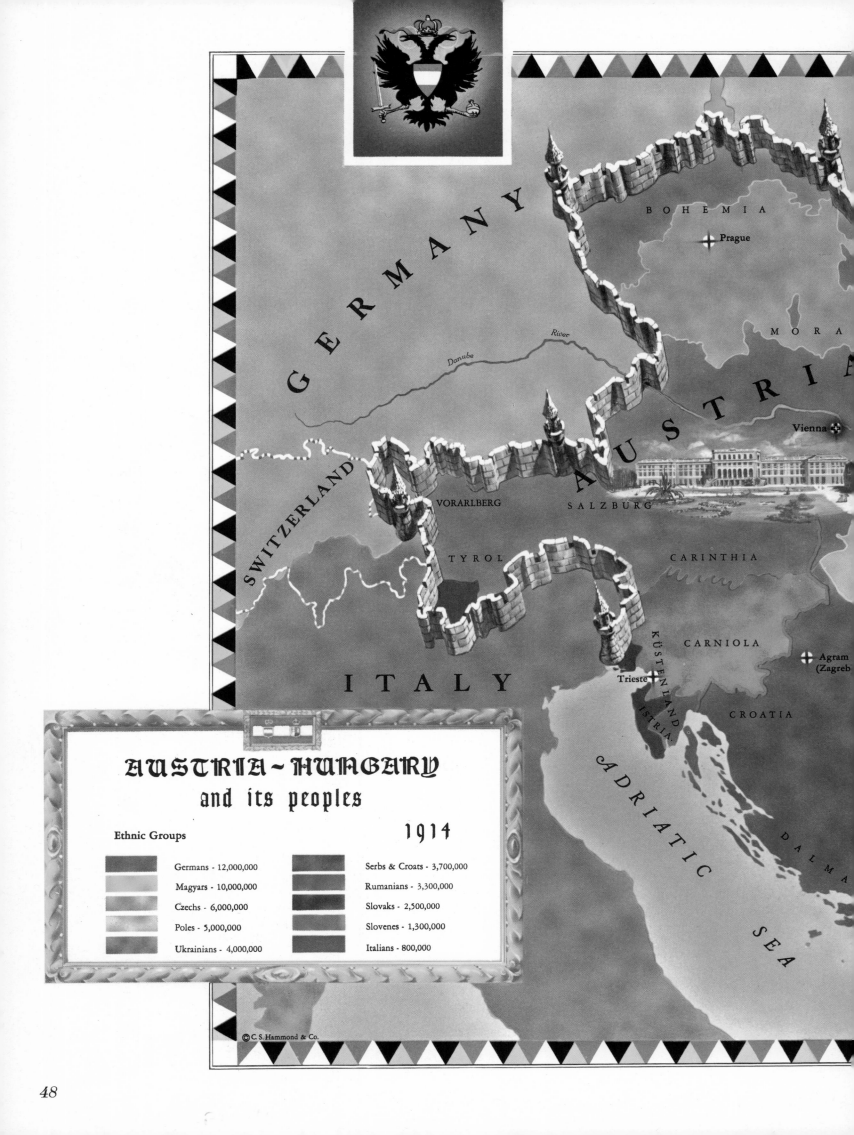

BOHEMIA

Prague

MORA

GERMANY

AUSTRIA

Danube River

Vienna

SWITZERLAND

VORARLBERG

SALZBURG

CARINTHIA

TYROL

CARNIOLA

Agram (Zagreb

Trieste

KÜSTENLAND

ISTRIA

CROATIA

ITALY

ADRIATIC

DALMA

SEA

AUSTRIA ~ HUNGARY
and its peoples

Ethnic Groups

1914

Germans - 12,000,000

Serbs & Croats - 3,700,000

Magyars - 10,000,000

Rumanians - 3,300,000

Czechs - 6,000,000

Slovaks - 2,500,000

Poles - 5,000,000

Slovenes - 1,300,000

Ukrainians - 4,000,000

Italians - 800,000

© C. S. Hammond & Co.

RUSSIAN EMPIRE

POLAND

GALICIA

+ Cracow

+ Lemberg

ESIA

Czernowitz

HUNGARY

BUKOVINA

+ Budapest

TRANSYLVANIA

+ Szeged

SLAVONIA

BANAT

RUMANIA

BOSNIA

+ Belgrade

Sarajevo
June 28, 1914

SERBIA

Danube   River

HERZEGOVINA

MONTENEGRO

BULGARIA

ALBANIA

Scale of Miles

0   50   100   150   200

Rocking the throne, *needy workers protest at Austria's Parliament*

In riots over the votes, *police ride down an angry Viennese mob*

How poor the poor? *A peasant farmhouse in Hapsburg's Croatia at the turn of the century*

A tattered Bosnian peasant carries his richest possession—a ram

When Franz Josef became Emperor of Austria in 1848, a revolutionary fire was spreading in Europe. Even the ancient throne of the Hapsburgs was not safe. Hungary, Bohemia, and the Italian provinces were in open revolt against imperial rule and against the economic feudalism that had kept the populace in a perpetual state of serfdom. Eventually, aided by an anxious Tsar, Franz Josef crushed the rebels and restored stern absolutism to his unhappy realm. But through his long reign, unrest—sometimes explosive, sometimes simmering—plagued the Emperor. In the distant provinces, nationalists churned the patriotic fervor of the repressed minorities. In Vienna, the partisans of democracy, socialism, anarchy, and anti-Semitism whipped up the impoverished urban workers. Finally, in the '90s, imperial power buckled under in bloody rioting over demands for universal suffrage. For almost a decade Franz Josef temporized. At last, in 1905, fearing a popular uprising similar to the one then sweeping Russia, he yielded. But it was too late. For the Hapsburgs and Imperial Austria-Hungary, the handwriting was on the wall.

The Fatal Moment

If Sarajevo had been the only personal tragedy in his life, Franz Josef might have restrained, at least temporarily, the martial forces unleashed in Austria by the assassination of Archduke Franz Ferdinand, his nephew and heir apparent. But he had endured too many tragedies. His younger brother, Emperor Maximilian I of Mexico, had been executed by a revolutionary firing squad; his only son, Crown Prince Rudolf, was the nineteenth century's most famous love suicide; and the Emperor's lovely wife, Elizabeth, had been fatally stabbed by an assassin in Geneva in 1898. And so, by 1914, the benevolent old autocrat was too weary, too detached, too long on the throne to do anything but mutter pious warnings about the calamity that lay ahead.

Franz Josef would live another two years and Austria-Hungary would survive until 1918, but the last chapter in the long history of the Hapsburg Empire was really written on that June day in Sarajevo. The moment the trigger was pulled, the empire was through.

The target: *Archduke Franz Ferdinand, and his wife*

The bullet: *On June 28, 1914, the Archduke was slain*

With Emperor Franz Josef and Kaiser Wilhelm II looking on, the Austrian cavalry rehearses for war

The era ended, the Emperor mourned his heir

The Giant Called Russia

While the momentous events in Europe were holding center stage, in the wings to the east, the enormous, brooding hulk of Russia was slowly and painfully rousing herself. Peter the Great, almost single-handedly, ruthlessly wrenched her from medievalism and established Russia as part of the Western world. Exploiting a fabulous store of timber, minerals, and grain, the Tsar's Russia expanded west and south and east for land and seaports. Such was Imperial Russia's power that a Moscow professor could exult: "Is there anything the Russian state could not do? A word —and a whole empire ceases to exist, a word—and another disappears from the face of the earth!" Napoleon attacked. Russia shrugged him off and emerged with international prestige, her borders surrounding fully one-eighth of the land surface of the

The spring thaw breaks the harsh winter's hold on Russia's heartland, the Ukraine

earth—a proud and imperialistic nation, governed absolutely by the Romanoff Tsars.

Yet behind the power and the glory of the Romanoff dynasty—beneath the dazzling wealth and glitter of the royal court—Mother Russia suffered a mortal illness. For Russia's strength was founded on her peasantry—the serfs who cut the forests, dug the coal, and reaped the wheat. And the dark, amorphous mass of 47 million peasants—the hidden, underwater mass of the shining Russian iceberg—lived in abject poverty, enduring incredible hardships. Ironically, in the Ukraine, at once the black-dirt breadbasket and the cradle of Russia, the plight of the peasant was worst: He lived in hovels, survived on a bare subsistence diet, and was taxed unmercifully—separated by an abyss from the gay life at court that he supported. It was his seething misery that would fan the wildfire of revolution against the jewel-bedecked princelings at the court in St. Petersburg.

Surrounded by prelates *of the Orthodox Church, Nicholas takes communion at his coronation*

Tsar Nicholas II, *the last of his line*

"Autocracy, orthodoxy, and nationalism," Tsar Nicholas I had thundered; and the watchwords reflected perfectly the sentiments of his great-grandson, Nicholas II, the last of the Romanoffs. Though personally pleasant enough, Nicholas was a narrow-minded autocrat who believed firmly in the divine right of kings, totally oblivious to the needs of his people and his time. Politically weak and inconsistent, he became increasingly dependent on his strong-willed wife, the Tsarina, who in turn was influenced by the strange religious figure, the monk Rasputin. In his world of privilege and established order, as his reign wore on, Nicholas II was pathetically unprepared to cope with—or to even sense—the winds of change that were sweeping across the steppes.

Nicholas' daughters (1913), Maria, Tatiana, Anastasia, Olga

Tsarina Alexandra, a strong-willed beauty with a fascination for the mystic

Nicholas' coronation celebration lit up Moscow; the Kremlin is in the background across the Moskva River

The key to Tsarist authority was the fierce, audacious army of Cossacks. The descendants of refugees from the kingdoms of Muscovy and Poland, the Cossacks established communities in the Dnieper and Don River basins. Bold, fiery, and brilliant soldiers, Cossack horsemen lived for fighting and knew no landlord master. They sallied forth from their Ukrainian strongholds for whichever ruler suited their interests of the moment—the King of Poland, the Sultan of Turkey, or the Tsar of Muscovy. Later, settling on the border steppes, they defended their communities—and in a larger sense, Russia herself—from the golden Tartar horde and all other comers. Though their ancestors were serfs, the Cossacks came to despise the peasants; and once absorbed into the gentry, became the Tsars' most efficient instrument for suppressing discontent. On the sturdy steeds and sharp lances of the hated Cossack cavalry rested the power of Tsarist Russia.

anging along the frontier, the intrepid, mobile Cossack force played a major role in Russia's expansion—a movement of breathtaking scope. In the north, Russia drove to the Arctic, enveloping Finland; in the west, she conquered most of Poland; in the south the Caspian and Black Seas were secured; and in the east, the Trans-Siberian railroad snaked across the steppes and deserts to the Pacific where Russia came up against a formidable adversary determined to check her influence in the Far East—Japan.

Crack Cossack cavalry *spearheaded the armies of the Tsar*

Circassian Cossack, *a haughty member of the Tsar's personal escort*

THE TSARIST EMPIRE IN THE 1900'S

The Russian Empire in 1900	Areas lost to Japan in 1905
Russian Spheres of Influence	Settled areas of the Russian Empire

POLAR PACK ICE

ALASKA
(U.S.)

BERING

SEA

ARCTIC OCEAN

River

ARCTIC CIRCLE

Kamchatka Peninsula

SEA OF

OKHOTSK

Lena

SIBERIA

Sakhalin

Kurile Islands (Jap.)

PACIFIC

Railway

Approximately 6000 miles

Lake
Baikal

from St. Petersburg to Vladivostok

Amur River

Chinese Eastern

Russian domination
of Manchuria-
to 1905

OCEAN

Railway

Vladivostok

SEA OF

JAPAN

Russian economic
domination of Mongolia-
after 1850

MONGOLIA

MANCHURIA

JAPAN

Tokyo

EMPIRE

Mukden

Russian economic
penetration of Korea
1896-1905

KOREA

Peking

Port Arthur
(Russian)

Tsushima Strait

YELLOW

SEA

COMPARATIVE SIZES OF THE RUSSIAN
EMPIRE AND THE UNITED STATES

6000 miles

United States-3,022,000 Square miles
Russian Empire-8,660,000 Square miles

Ethnic Groups

Great Russians-55,700,000   Germans-1,800,000
Ukrainians-22,400,000   Jews-5,100,000
White Russians-5,900,000   Finns-2,500,000
Poles-7,900,000   Estonians-1,000,000
Lithuanians-1,700,000   Kirghiz-4,300,000
Letts-1,400,000   Tatars-3,800,000
Iranians-800,000   Mongols-500,000
Armenians-1,200,000   Georgians-1,400,000
Rumanians-1,100,000   Others-9,800,000

0   250   500   750   1000

Scale   of   Miles

THE CLASH
OF INTERESTS

SPHERES OF INFLUENCE

Russian

Japanese

Scale of Miles
0   200   400   600

B y the end of the nineteenth century, Japan had become a formidable rival indeed. Under Emperor Mutsuhito, the Japanese Empire was created in a single generation. To the north, Japan annexed the Kuriles; to the south and east, the Ryukyus, the Bonins, the Volcanoes, and Marcus Island. After her victorious war against China in 1894-95, the Japanese occupied Taiwan and the Pescadores; Korea became a vassal. Yet, always — across the Sea of Japan — loomed the menacing specter of Russia. From Tokyo's point of view, Russia's imperialistic intentions were obvious: They coincided exactly with her own. In 1900, the Boxer Rebellion provided Russia with the excuse to send troops to Manchuria. When Russia refused to pull out, Japan's course was clear—and the fate of the Far East for years to come was thus decided. With England's tacit approval, the Imperial Japanese Staff prepared its bold plans. And at dawn, Feb. 6, 1904, Admiral Togo signaled his superbly disciplined fleet: "We sail this morning. Our enemy flies the Russian flag."

Flagship of the Russian Baltic Fleet, the Suvoroff led the epic 20,000 mile voyage to the Far East

Getting up steam *in Port Arthur, Russian dreadnaughts prepared to meet the attacking Japanese fleet*

Striking as stealthily as it did 37 years later at Pearl Harbor, the Japanese Fleet shelled Russian men-of-war moored at Port Arthur in Manchuria. For months, the Russian ships remained close to protective shore batteries, but Togo's guns and the artillery of the advancing Japanese army whittled down the Russian Fleet, and Port Arthur fell. Meanwhile, Tsar Nicholas II ordered the Baltic Fleet to the Far East. In an ill-starred yet magnificent voyage that captured the world's imagination, Admiral Rozhdestvenski in the battleship Suvoroff led his yellow-funnelled warships around Africa, bound for Vladivostok. Onward, through the China Sea, he steamed, toward Tsushima Strait—where Togo's ambush waited.

THE LONG VOYAGE
Route of the Russian Baltic Fleet
Main Fleet ⟶   Reinforcements ⇢

Japan Looms Up

Russia and the rest of the world had grossly underestimated the new Japan. All had failed to see behind the feudal habits that clung to the busy island people. Actually, the Japanese had performed a miracle in Westernizing the nation—industrially and militarily—in a handful of years. Japan, in 1639, had closed her doors with the imperial edict: "In the future, and for as long as the sun shall continue to light the world, let no man attempt to land in Japan, even as an ambassador; and let this order never be infringed, on pain of death." The Land of the Rising Sun remained in medieval isolation until Commodore Matthew B. Perry's historic visit in 1853 opened her doors again. During the long reign, from 1867 to 1912, of Emperor Mutsuhito—known as the Meiji (enlightened government) Era— Japan's progress was startling. She leaped boldly forward into the modern world; her political, economic, and intellectual life was shaped in a Western mold with the Emperor as the symbol and inspiration of the new Japanese spirit.

In the style of a Japanese print, at the turn of the century

from the top:
Old and new fashions in Tokyo,

A Japanese aristocrat's home,

First streetlight illuminates Tokyo,

A Japanese fire brigade hard at work

← _____

The progressive Emperor Mutsuhito *portrayed against a sand-wave garden background*

Patiently toiling at their reels in a silk mill, Japanese women provided the labor force for manufacturing plants

The vast shops of the Kawasaki Ship Building Co. turned out heavy-duty turbines that powered the nation's ships

The orderly, intelligent Japanese mastered the Western man's machines with amazing thoroughness. They learned to send silk out into the world to trade for the things their imperial overlords needed for industrial expansion—mostly expansion for war. The new Japan had no intention of remaining in the background of the struggle for global power; Tokyo, by its Westernization, was bound to become the heart of an empire. Had the Russians not been so witless, they would have measured Japan's power and aims more accurately. Looking back, it seems possible that rapprochement in Asia might have saved Imperial Russia and only at the cost of some of her never-realized ambitions in the Orient.

Japanese industry, such as this electrical factory, quickly adopted Western mass-production techniques

With the growth of the new Japan came commerce, banking, railroads, communications, shipping, manufacturing, heavy industry—and schools. All things foreign were popular—even Western dress. Though some among the European nations might still scoff at her parrotry, as she tried to find herself in the modern world, a heady spirit of empire was fusing Japan and her people into a proud, cohesive, purposeful nation—ready and able to stand among the most powerful nations on the earth.

The huge Yawata Iron and Steel Mills in Kyushu provided bone and muscle for greater industrialization

POLAR PACK ICE

ARCTIC OCEAN

ARCTIC CIRCLE

BERING SEA

Kamchatka Peninsula

SEA OF OKHOTSK

Kurile Islands

Sakhalin

SIBERIA

Lena River

Czech Legions 1918

Lake Baikal

Semenov 1918

Amur River

MANCHURIA

Japanese 1920-1925

Ungern-Sternberg 1920-1921

Americans, British & Japanese 1918-1920

Vladivostok

MONGOLIA

Americans & British 1918-1920

Japanese 1918-1922

CHINA

CHOSEN (KOREA)

JAPAN

Reds had spread terror over all of Russia. The Whites struck back savagely, but to no avail. So Russia went the full circle—from Tsarist to Communist autocracy—while the world presumably was being made safe for democracy.

LEGEND

Soviet-stronghold at the beginning of the Civil War–1918

Allied intervention–1918-1925

White Army offensives–1918-1922

Soviet counter-offensives–1918-1922

Areas lost by Russia after the October Revolution–1917

Scale of Miles

0   200   400   600   800   1000

81

On a triumphant European tour, *President Wilson rides through Rome*

"The world must be made safe for Democracy."

Woodrow Wilson, 1917

The World of Idealism and Upheaval

If Queen Victoria had indomitably stood for the nineteenth century's world of imperialism ruled by the colonial powers of Europe, the twentieth century's spirit of idealism was symbolized in the person of one man: Woodrow Wilson, 28th President of the United States.

When Wilson took office in 1913, the republic was cresting an unprecedented wave of national well-being. By the turn of the century, the frontier had nearly vanished. As America's wealth and power increased so did her confidence; and, after years of self-imposed isolation, the nation seemed ready to meet her destiny in world affairs. Such was the country's buoyant mood when Wilson was inaugurated with his program, "The New Freedom."

Intelligent, informed, and eloquent, Wilson came to the Presidency with great gifts. He also brought a streak of self-righteousness that left no room for compromise, which would prove a tragic flaw. As a college professor, the President had been a close student of constitutional government and he guided an impressive program of domestic legislation through Congress. But it was in a larger role that history was to judge him. In 1917, the United States declared war.

To most Americans, the war was an almost light-hearted affair, a time of patriotic fervor—of Liberty Loans, Yeomanettes, and gasless Sundays. As the bands played "Over There," the doughboys marched jauntily off to war; and in bloody battles with strange names like Château-Thierry, St. Mihiel, and Belleau Wood, they fought and died. Though Wilson abhorred the conflict, he was sustained by his firm conviction that from the nettle, war, he could pluck the flower, peace. As a basis for a just settlement, he proposed his Fourteen Points, to which millions of the earth's peoples responded enthusiastically. And at the close of the war Wilson declared hopefully: "The fortunes of mankind are now in the hands of the plain people of the world."

At one minute to 11 on the cold, foggy morning of Nov. 11, 1918, the last French "75" had thundered on its carriage, then all, suddenly, was quiet on the Western front. The war to end all wars was over. The armistice touched off a delirious celebration, and the boys came marching home. America's spirits were high: The nation's armies were victorious, her prestige was unsurpassed in the chancelleries of the world, and her President prepared to

negotiate a lasting peace. But in Europe, the armistice brought
the terrible realization that World War I was the war that nobody
won and everyone lost. Four years of carnage had bled Europe
white: Britain, France, Italy, Russia, Germany, and Austria-
Hungary had lost millions of men. The continent was shell-shocked.
The old order lay in ruins, never to be the same. And the inevitable disillusionment was setting in.

For the Kaiser's son *there would be no throne*

For the defeated Kaiser, *exile in Holland*

Germans starved, *and men and women alike were reduced to scavenging for stray potatoes*

A strange sight, French occupation troops arrive in Berlin

A city in turmoil, Germans battle Germans in Berlin's streets

What came to Europe with the end of hostilities was not so much peace as turmoil. The Kaiser and his family were forced to flee to Holland, after German revolutionaries demanded a peace settlement. In a subsequent struggle for power, rival Socialist parties brought Germany to the brink of disaster. During the war, half of the nation's livestock and 40 per cent of the crops had been lost. Unheedingly, the Allies continued their strangling food blockade. Hundreds of thousands of Germans starved to death in the bitter winter of 1918-19. In Central European cities, extremist groups took over; various ethnic and national groups clashed over boundaries. Everywhere, dizzying inflation wiped out savings. As disorder spread, the very fabric of European society seemed to be disintegrating. In desperation, the continent looked for stability to the statesmen and politicians gathering at Versailles.

Clemenceau, *the Tiger of France, fought tooth and claw to crush Germany forever*

The Men and Meeting at Versailles

In the thickly carpeted, ornately furnished rooms of Louis XIV's Versailles Palace, the Allied delegates buckled down to work. The peace conference was dominated by the Big Four: The tall, aloof Wilson; suave, adroit Lloyd George of England; affable Orlando of Italy; and wily, old Clemenceau, the Tiger of France. From the first, the conference was marked by a dramatic duel between two strong personalities: The American President vs. the French Premier. To Wilson, Clemenceau seemed a cynical champion of the old order whose only concern was one of narrow-minded self-interest. To Clemenceau, who twice in his lifetime had seen his country overrun by Germans, Wilson was a well-meaning but naïve visionary, totally un-aware of the facts of European political life.

Week after week the peacemakers haggled, but in session after session bitter compromises were made, and the delegates hammered out the Treaty of Versailles. The final version really satisfied no one: Wilsonian idealists thought it too hard on the defeated nations; others, who favored Clemenceau's program for crippling Germany, thought it too soft. Certainly, Germany was deeply embittered by its crushing reparations obligations. With grim foresight, Gen. Tasker H. Bliss, American delegation member, observed: "Why deceive ourselves? We are making no peace here." Yet Wilson had what he wanted most: A provision for a League of Nations firmly written into the treaty.

June 28, 1919: *In the magnificent Hall of Mirrors, the Allies signed the fateful Treaty of Versailles with Germany*

In his fight against isolationism, President Wilson arrives in St. Paul to speak for the League of Nations

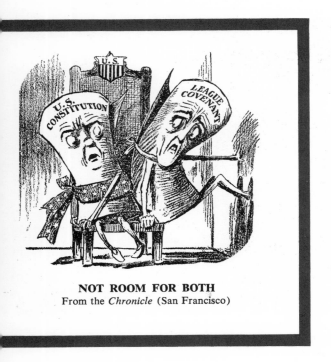

NOT ROOM FOR BOTH
From the *Chronicle* (San Francisco)

resident Wilson sailed for the United States, confident the Senate would quickly ratify the peace treaty. But powerful opposition had been forming led by such formidable Republican senators as William Borah of Idaho, Hiram Johnson of California, and, most important, Henry Cabot Lodge, the shrewd chairman of the Foreign Relations Committee. Wilson deeply believed that the weaknesses of the Versailles Treaty made it imperative that the nation join the League of Nations; the fight for ratification, therefore, became a struggle to bring America into the League. Had Wilson been willing to conciliate, he might have gotten most of what he wanted; but, to Wilson, compromise was unthinkable. Instead, he felt that his foes were no more than a "little group of willful men." The President had been counting on an aroused nation to carry the day. But many Americans were genuinely confused about the issues, and the

In the fight for isolationism, Wilson's foe, Henry Cabot Lodge, with Elihu Root, the League proponent

President had done precious little to enlighten them. As Senate resistance hardened, so did Wilson's determination to make no compromises. The President decided to rally public opinion behind him through an extensive speaking tour. During the grueling trip through the west, the 63-year-old chief executive grew increasingly exhausted, until he finally collapsed after speaking in Colorado. Never again was the President a well man, and all effective support for the League dissipated. The Senate summarily rejected the Versailles pact; not until 1921 did it ratify a separate peace with the Central Powers. Thus, Woodrow Wilson's dreams for American membership in the League of Nations were shattered on the anvil of his intransigence. As his administration ended, he said prophetically: "We had a chance to gain the leadership of the world. We have lost it, and soon we shall be witnessing the tragedy of it all."

HANGING UP THE MAILED FIST

FRANCE AND GERMANY: 'Will that nail be strong enough?'
ENGLAND (in the rear): 'It all depends upon the man with the hammer.'
From News of the World (London)

ATLANTIC OCEAN

North Sea

NORWAY

SWEDEN

FINLAND

R U

IRISH FREE STATE

UNITED KINGDOM

DENMARK

ESTONIA

Baltic Sea

LATVIA

LITHUANIA

NETHERLANDS

BELGIUM

LUX.

SAAR

GERMANY

POLAND

St. Germain
Neuilly
Trianon
Sèvres
Versailles

CZECHOSLOVAKIA

Lausanne

LIECHTENSTEIN

SWITZERLAND

AUSTRIA

HUNGARY

RUMANIA

FRANCE

ANDORRA

SAN MARINO

MONACO

PORTUGAL

SPAIN

Corsica
(French)

ITALY

Adriatic Sea

YUGOSLAVIA

BULGARIA

Bla

T U

Balearic Is.
(Sp.)

Sardinia
(Italian)

ALBANIA

TANGIER
(International)

GIBRALTAR
(British)

Mediterranean

GREECE

SPANISH MOROCCO

Sicily
(Italian)

Malta (Br.)

Dodecanese
(It.)

MOROCCO
(French)

ALGERIA
(French)

TUNISIA
(French)

Sea

Crete
(Greek)

LIBYA

EGY

The Old Empires

		Area (square miles)	Population
GERMANY	Prewar	208,780	65 million
	Postwar	180,822	61 million
RUSSIA	Prewar	8,660,000	182 million
	Postwar	8,300,000	158 million
AUSTRIA-HUNGARY	Prewar	261,029	51 million
	Postwar	32,369 (Austria)	6 million (Austria)
		35,875 (Hungary)	8 million (Hungary)
TURKEY	Prewar	710,224	20 million
	Postwar	294,500	13 million

(In addition, Germany lost her overseas territories--area, 1,023,347; population, 12 million.)

The New Republics

	Area (square miles)	Population
CZECHOSLOVAKIA	54,246	13.6 million
POLAND	150,056	27 million
YUGOSLAVIA (monarchy)	95,578	12 million
FINLAND	146,915	3.3 million
ESTONIA	18,353	1 million
LATVIA	24,440	1.5 million
LITHUANIA	20,500	2 million
IRISH FREE STATE	26,601	3 million

Other Major Territorial Changes

		Area (square miles)	Population
FRANCE	Prewar	207,000	39.6 million
	Postwar	212,741	40 million
ITALY	Prewar	110,623	35 million
	Postwar	120,000	39 million
RUMANIA	Prewar	52,760	7.6 million
	Postwar	122,000	15 million

(In addition, small border changes increased the size of Belgium, Denmark and Greece, decreased the area of Bulgaria. The Arab lands, other than independent Saudi Arabia, which were taken from the Ottoman Empire were placed under British and French mandate.)

This Was Self-Determination

Even before the last cannon was fired on the Western front, a vast wave of change swept Eastern Europe, destroying the old order. The violent surge of nationalism among the oppressed minorities redrew the boundaries of the Hapsburg Empire, presenting the peacemakers in Paris with a *fait accompli* they could do little more than ratify. To the north, Finland and the Baltic states took advantage of the Russian civil war to break the yoke of Romanoff domination. In all, seven new European states joined the family of nations. These were the real victors, and their new freedom represented a great advance for Wilson's most cherished principle—the self-determination of nations. But if, on balance, the new boundaries were more just than the old, they also contained serious inequities—inequities which would keep alive smoldering resentments for decades to come.

Czech Foreign Minister, Eduard Beneš

President Masaryk of Czechoslovakia

Ignace Paderewski, Polish Premier

New Boundaries, New Leaders

The redrawing of boundaries was not a cure-all for what troubled the chaotic Eastern half of Europe. Freedom in itself was not enough. The old enmities were too deep-rooted. The minorities, though now free of Hapsburg domination, were still not free of their historic mistrust of each other. Only inspired and farsighted leadership could bring stability —and a lasting peace to the Balkans.

The new leaders who now emerged were as diverse in background, temperament, and political philosophy as in the languages they spoke. Poland's new Premier was her beloved, idealistic Ignace Paderewski, the world's foremost pianist; in Hungary, Adm. Nicholas Horthy led a reign of terror which overthrew a short-lived Communist regime and became his country's strong man; in Belgrade, Prince Regent Alexander of Serbia mounted to a new throne as King of Yugoslavia; in Athens, a master of intrigue and seasoned politician, Premier Eleutherios Venizelos, embarked on an ambitious program of expansion at the expense of defeated Turkey only to see his dream shattered by the force of Turkish arms under the able, ruthless Mustafa Kemal.

In the new republics, one leader towered over the rest in worldwide esteem—Thomas Masaryk, philosopher and teacher, who with the help of his disciple, Eduard Beneš, brought stability and respect to Czechoslovakia. The son of a coachman and a servant girl, it was Masaryk's dream to make his little state a pilot plant, a showcase for democracy. In large measure he succeeded, but, despite his efforts, the old enmities did not die. The Balkans remained as explosive and unstable as they had been when under Hapsburg domination.

Father of modern Turkey, Mustafa Kemal

Greece's anti-royalist, Premier Venizelos

Hungary's strong man, Admiral Horthy

A king enthroned, Alexander of Yugoslavia

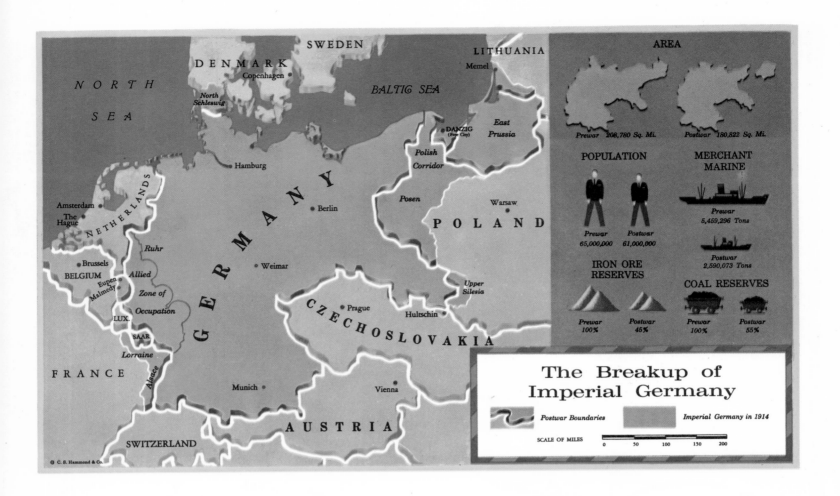

AREA

Prewar 208,780 Sq. Mi.   Postwar 180,822 Sq. Mi.

POPULATION

Prewar 65,000,000   Postwar 61,000,000

MERCHANT MARINE

Prewar 5,459,296 Tons

Postwar 2,590,073 Tons

IRON ORE RESERVES

Prewar 100%   Postwar 45%

COAL RESERVES

Prewar 100%   Postwar 55%

The Breakup of Imperial Germany

Postwar Boundaries   Imperial Germany in 1914

SCALE OF MILES
0   50   100   150   200

© C. S. Hammond & Co.

The Breakup of the Austro-Hungarian Empire

Austria-Hungary in 1914
Postwar Boundaries

SCALE OF MILES
0   50   100   200   300   400

© C. S. Hammond & Co.

For the losers, it was a humiliating peace. In physical terms, Germany was dealt a crushing blow. But it was not merely the material loss which made Versailles such a bitter peace. Of all the treaty provisions, the one that rankled the most was the "war guilt" clause which forced the Germans to admit that they alone had been responsible for the war. Even as the treaty was being signed, one German publication exhorted the people: "Do not lose hope. The resurrection day comes."

The treaties for Austria and Hungary were modeled on Versailles, even to the point of demanding crushing reparations. Neither had any ability to pay; they barely had the means of feeding themselves. As a way out of her troubles, Austria asked to be allowed to join Germany. This the Allies refused to consider —a defeated Germany was not to be rewarded with territorial gains.

Of the defeated powers, Turkey fared the best. The treaty of Sèvres was as crushing as Versailles, but it never went into effect. It was rewritten with Turkish blood. Mustafa Kemal defeated the Greeks in a fierce, no-quarter fight and forced the signing of a new treaty. Turkey lost only Arab territories, and she had held them only loosely.

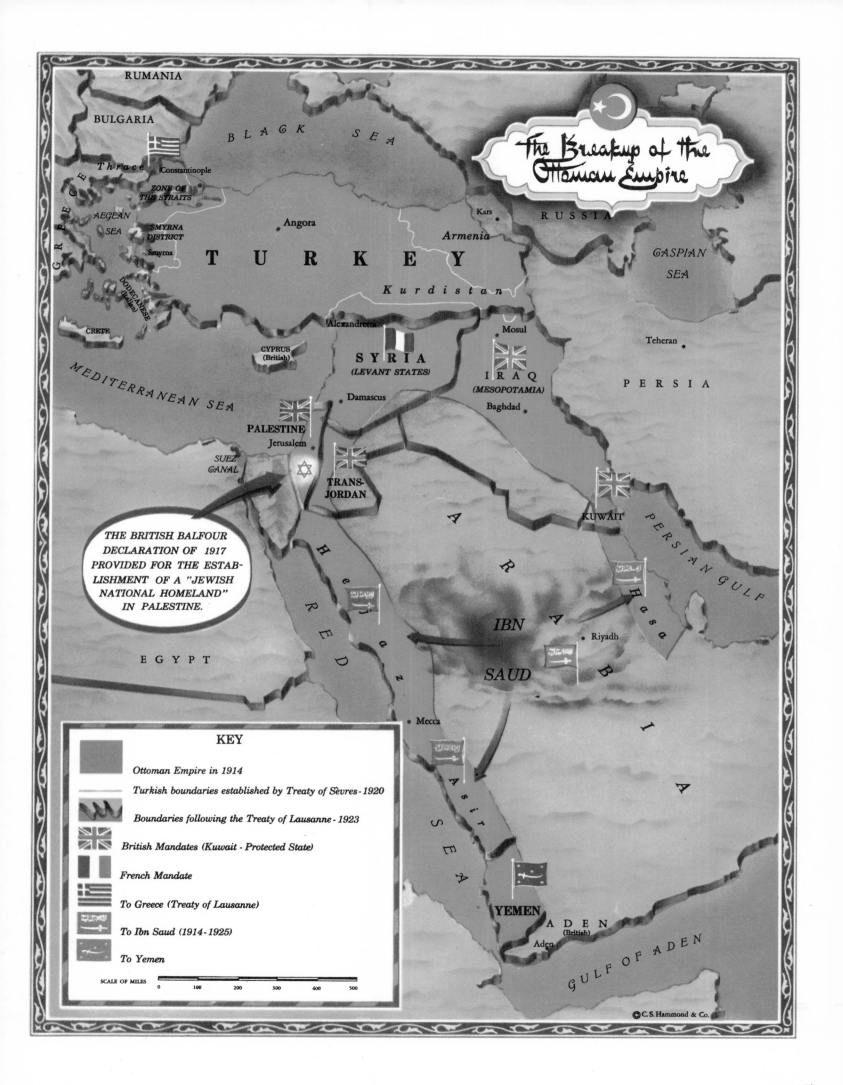

The Breakup of the Ottoman Empire

RUMANIA
BULGARIA
BLACK SEA
RUSSIA
Thrace
Constantinople
ZONE OF THE STRAITS
AEGEAN SEA
SMYRNA DISTRICT
Smyrna
DODECANESE (Italian)
CRETE
Angora
T U R K E Y
Kars
Armenia
Kurdistan
CASPIAN SEA

MEDITERRANEAN SEA
Alexandretta
CYPRUS (British)
SYRIA (LEVANT STATES)
Damascus
Mosul
IRAQ (MESOPOTAMIA)
Baghdad
PERSIA
Teheran

PALESTINE
Jerusalem
SUEZ CANAL
TRANS-JORDAN

THE BRITISH BALFOUR DECLARATION OF 1917 PROVIDED FOR THE ESTABLISHMENT OF A "JEWISH NATIONAL HOMELAND" IN PALESTINE.

EGYPT
He j a z
R E D
Hasa
KUWAIT
PERSIAN GULF
A R A B I A
IBN SAUD
Riyadh

Mecca

Asir
S E A

YEMEN
ADEN (British)
Aden
GULF OF ADEN

KEY

Ottoman Empire in 1914

Turkish boundaries established by Treaty of Sèvres - 1920

Boundaries following the Treaty of Lausanne - 1923

British Mandates (Kuwait - Protected State)

French Mandate

To Greece (Treaty of Lausanne)

To Ibn Saud (1914 - 1925)

To Yemen

SCALE OF MILES
0   100   200   300   400   500

© C. S. Hammond & Co.

97

The Death of a Dream

During his final 17 months in office, President Wilson was a virtual invalid, the victim of a cerebral stroke. For weeks at a time, he was unable to sign documents; his condition remained a mystery to the country; rumors spread; and the Senate went so far as to send a committee to the White House to ascertain whether the President was still mentally competent. Still, Wilson hung grimly on, hoping that the election of 1920 would serve as a "great and solemn referendum" to vindicate his faith in American participation in the League. Wilson's hopes were in vain. War and its aftermath had given America its fill of international responsibility. So, in the autumn of 1920, the people in overwhelming numbers turned away from the Democratic party and the Wilsonian ideal of noble exertion. Instead, they chose a man who offered them complacency, relaxation, and "normalcy"—Warren Gamaliel Harding, the remarkably undistinguished Senator from Ohio.

Worn and ill, *President Wilson left office a defeated man*

Senators *Fall (left) and Hitchcock (right) leaving the White House after their extraordinary call on the sick President*

Harding and Coolidge; *on a platform of isolationism and 'normalcy,' the Republicans swept the election of 1920*

Mrs. Harding, *a powerful woman in the White House*

Warren Harding, and his running mate, Calvin Coolidge, the Massachusetts Governor who won his reputation by intervening in the Boston police strike, promised to deliver America from Woodrow Wilson and all his works. The Republican theme was in tune with the national temper—which had decided that foreign entanglements and the business of world leadership was sheer folly. Thus, the 1920s were to see America retiring into its shell as it "returned to normalcy." Harding's conception of the Presidency was a modest one: He was a spokesman for policies determined by others, a guest of honor at such ceremonial functions as the opening of public buildings. He named strong men like Charles Evans Hughes, State; Andrew Mellon, Treasury; and Herbert Hoover, Commerce. But to other posts, he named political hacks, "The Ohio Gang," who blackened the name of his administration with their crimes. Behind the scenes, the First Lady herself played favorites and meddled in White House politics. President Harding died in San Francisco, and there are those who say until this day that he died of a "broken heart" because of the scandals involving his Ohio "friends."

After a long legal battle that stirred the world Nicola Sacco and Bartolomeo Vanzetti were executed

The Era of Anti-'Radicalism' . . .

America's idealistic wartime adventure brought a violent reaction against all things "alien," "radical," and "bolshevik." Attorney General Palmer led mass arrests of aliens with small regard for constitutional safeguards. The *cause célèbre* of the time was the Sacco-Vanzetti case—the Italian anarchists who were executed for the murder of two men in Massachusetts. Though many thought that the evidence against the men was weak—

that they were convicted mainly because of their unpopular political beliefs—Sacco and Vanzetti did not die until seven years of hearings and appeals failed to clear them. For the most part, however, America did not concern herself with such "alien" affairs. These were the heady years of the "era of wonderful nonsense," the "roaring '20s," the "jazz age," and Americans were embarked on a monumental spree. Liquor was outlawed

Texas Guinan's nightclub was a New York landmark. Her famous greeting was, 'Hello, sucker'

New York's McSorley's *ale house bowed to the law but survived 'dry' days*

... And Nonsense

in 1919; the "noble experiment" of temperance advocates was on. But as one humorist of the day put it: "Then prohibition came along and everybody started to drink." The hip-flask, bathtub gin, and needled beer were the rage. The speakeasy became fashionable, the bootlegger indispensable, and millions flouted the law of the land. Gone were the days of national dedication, of Wilsonian idealism; America was living it up.

A Harding pair, *Daugherty (left), and Means*

Scandals of the '20s

Beneath the gaiety and good times, a deep malaise affected American life. Its extent could be seen in the nation's attitude toward the scandals of the Harding Administration. Frauds were uncovered in the Veterans' Bureau and in the Department of Justice; Attorney General Daugherty, an old crony of Harding's, was directly implicated. But the worst of the revelations was Teapot Dome, a barren tract of oil-rich land in Wyoming that had been reserved for future use by the Navy. In exchange for a "loan" of $100,000, Interior Secretary Fall leased the Teapot Dome and Elk Hills, Calif., reserves to his friends, the oil magnates Harry F. Sinclair and E. M. Doheny. After the investigations, all parties were thoroughly discredited; Fall was sent to prison for accepting a bribe. Sinclair and Doheny got off comparatively lightly and the country had the impression that the real malefactors were the ones who first exposed the whole sordid business. The Harding scandals caused a flurry of speculation about the late President, including *The Strange Death of President Harding,* a book by Gaston B. Means. A friend of Daugherty's and a notorious liar, Means implied that Mrs. Harding poisoned her husband. Such charges were never substantiated but it was symptomatic of the times that the allegations received serious consideration. Symptomatic, too, was the seeming indifference to the scandals: The public seemed to have lost its capacity for indignation.

Suffragette parader; in 1920 women finally won the right to vote, and the nation advanced steadily toward equality of the sexes

Silent Calvin Coolidge had become the 30th President of the United States by lamplight at his father's home in Vermont. He had seen to the firm prosecution of the Harding malefactors. Now came what seemed to be a golden age. The idols of the day were larger than life, legitimate objects of hero worship. Who could compare with a Ruth in baseball? A Dempsey in boxing, a Grange in football, a Jones in golf, or a Tilden in tennis? The great sporting contests were attended by thousands; and millions more heard the exciting play-by-play via the new scientific phenomenon, radio. In Hollywood, the stars of the silver screen shone with first-magnitude brilliance: Douglas Fairbanks, Mary Pickford, John Gilbert, Greta Garbo, Norma Talmadge, Charlie Chaplin. A black-faced entertainer named Al Jolson sang "Mammy" in "The Jazz Singer," and the talkies were born. When Rudolph Valentino, a dashing lover of the silent screen, died in New York in 1926, nearly 100,000 women mourned at his bier. Yet, if the '20s had more than their share of glamor, they had much more than their share of corruption. Thriving on illicit liquor profits, organized crime became big business. In many areas, gangsters rolled disdainfully through the streets in armored limousines, defying law and order with an impunity that amounted to a national disgrace.

A popular painting showed Coolidge being given the oath by his father

'Sultan of Swat': As the Babe swung mightily, thousands cheered

'Son of the Sheik': When Valentino waxed tender, thousands sighed softly

Gangsters ruled the cities like overlords. To reap the profits of prohibition, New York and Chicago were first divided like duchies of Europe, then consolidated—or conquered—and formed into rich kingdoms. The names on this map are the rulers, the areas their kingdoms.

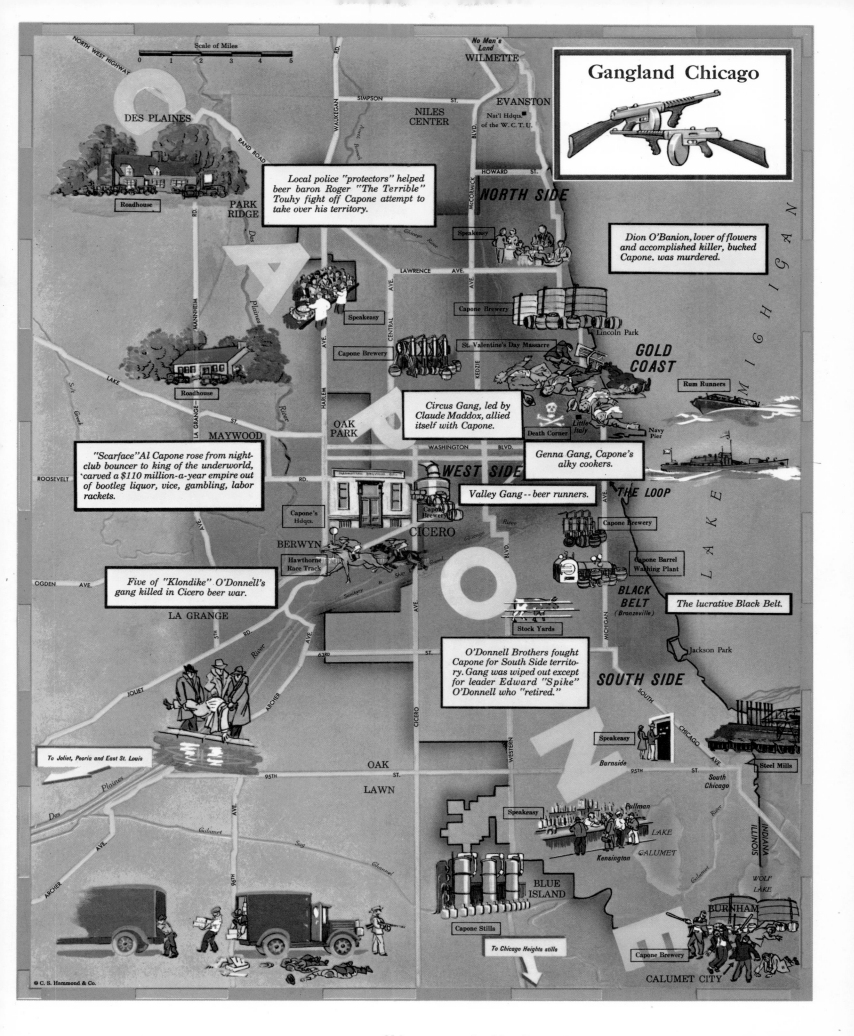

Gangland Chicago

Local police "protectors" helped beer baron Roger "The Terrible" Touhy fight off Capone attempt to take over his territory.

Dion O'Banion, lover of flowers and accomplished killer, bucked Capone, was murdered.

Circus Gang, led by Claude Maddox, allied itself with Capone.

"Scarface" Al Capone rose from night-club bouncer to king of the underworld, carved a $110 million-a-year empire out of bootleg liquor, vice, gambling, labor rackets.

Genna Gang, Capone's alky cookers.

Valley Gang -- beer runners.

Five of "Klondike" O'Donnell's gang killed in Cicero beer war.

The lucrative Black Belt.

O'Donnell Brothers fought Capone for South Side territory. Gang was wiped out except for leader Edward "Spike" O'Donnell who "retired."

Chicago was the bloodiest of prohibition's monarchies. There were many small kingdoms before Al Capone stepped to the top of a bloody pile to rule unchallenged until President Hoover saw to it that he went to prison. To this day, the mark of Capone is the shame of the city.

Clarence Darrow (left) chatting with William Jennings Bryan in the Dayton courtroom during the 'great monkey trial.' The defendant, Scopes (to right), was convicted of teaching evolution and fined $100

Outspoken champion of air power, Billy Mitchell was court-martialed for insubordination

In political outlook, America had retrenched, yet there was innovation in many fields. Great strides were taken in science and industry. In medicine and physics the revolutionary theories of Freud and Einstein were being put to work. In religion modern philosophical ideas challenged the beliefs of Fundamentalists; and the controversy was dramatically revealed when a Dayton, Tenn., high school teacher named John T. Scopes was charged with breaking a state law by teaching the theory of evolution. In the trial's circus-like atmosphere, the press led by Henry L. Mencken regaled the nation with the spectacle of William Jennings Bryan defending the literal interpretation of the Bible against the attack of Clarence Darrow, on behalf of science. The Scopes trial and Col. Billy Mitchell's court-martial for his vigorous advocacy of military air forces, were the dramatic moments while America really got rolling into the automobile age and a search for more rainbows. And the great Florida boom then seemed very close to the end of another rainbow.

This 'Model T,' *a 1921 product of Henry Ford, was followed by millions more that turned America into a nation on wheels*

During the '20s, *America went off on a huge binge, and one aspect of the national madness was the Charleston*

In the great *abortive Florida land boom, Coral Gables offered free transportation to a dreamland in the sun*

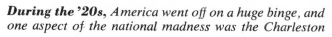

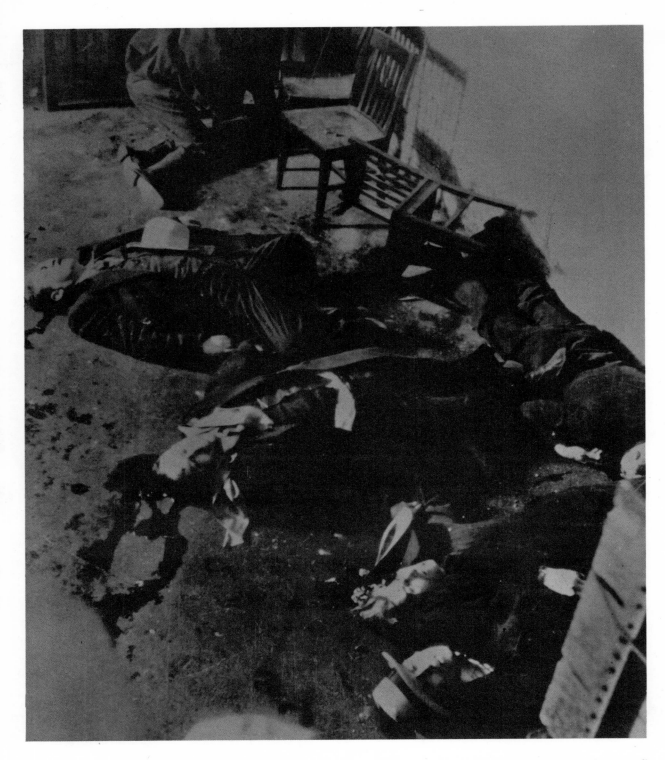

St. Valentine's Day, Chicago; *lined up against a garage wall, seven men were 'executed'*

Lawlessness grew far beyond the business of peddling bad whiskey and bad beer to willing buyers. Murder came wholesale. In Chicago alone, there were more than 500 killings, nearly all unsolved. Al Capone, foremost practitioner of the art, made millions; and not until 1931, was he imprisoned; and then, not for murder, but merely income tax evasion. All the bloodshed, though, had not quite prepared Chicago for St. Valentine's Day 1929, when seven gangsters were machine-gunned to death by a rival mob. For sheer indifference to human life, that massacre was the sorry climax. The bubbly effervescence of the era of wonderful nonsense was going stale. The country was waking up to the price of prohibition, but it did not know then that the end of prohibition would only mean a greater price; a gangster invasion of politics (as in New York), of labor, and, indeed, of legitimate business of all kinds.

Road Signs Marked Disaster

To America, Europe once again seemed very far away, but while America once again turned her eyes inward and readopted her traditional pose of isolationism, events in Europe were taking place which would soon have dire consequences in Washington as well as in Berlin, Rome, London, and Paris. For the defeated, of course, the war had been disastrous, but, after the first wave of exultation, the victors, too, found that peace had not brought the utopia their leaders had promised.

The war had destroyed the very economic fabric of the whole continent. No nation did not feel the pinch of poverty; no nation did not feel she had been treated unfairly at the conference tables. Because of this misery and discontent, men everywhere began to be infected with the revolutionary virus of Communism on the left, Fascism on the right, and great areas of the world which Wilson had hoped to make safe for democracy ran headlong down the road toward totalitarianism.

Mounted police *disperse London mob during general strike in 1926*

With the help *of volunteers, the government soon broke the strike*

German artist *Kaethe Kollwitz movingly portrayed Europe's sorrows—here, 'The Unemployed'*

With the drastic drop in world trade, unemployment rose in England. Hit hardest were miners. The growing use of new fuels and the great depth of mines long worked made British coal uneconomic. The government decided to close some mines, decree longer hours in the others. At this, the powerful Trades Union Congress called upon all union members to strike. Here was anarchy. But in a few days, the bitter general strike was broken. In England, at least, constitutional government had survived.

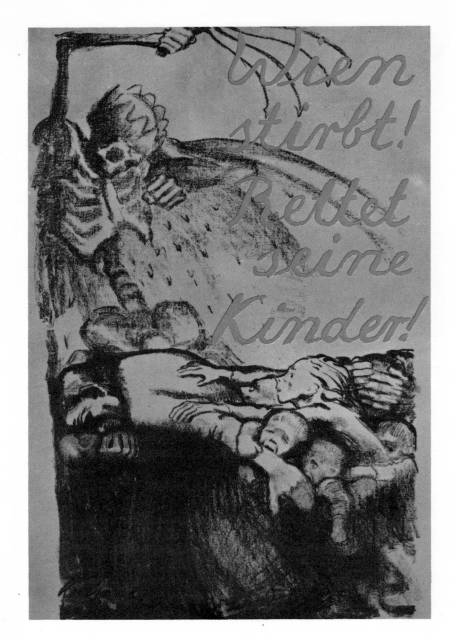

"Vienna is dying! Save its children!" Nowhere was there greater misery than in the former seat of the Hapsburgs. Vienna, the proudest jewel of the old empire, was now starving. Other areas were nearly as hard hit. In country after country, runaway inflation destroyed savings, made currency worth less than the paper it was printed on. As the decade wore on conditions would gradually improve, but millions would not share in the new gains, and for others, the recovery would come too late.

The plight of Vienna's children, a lithograph by Kollwitz

The women of Vienna search for food in city dump

As the Spirit of St. Louis winged across the Atlantic, a waiting world
offered prayers for the safety of the Lone Eagle, Charles A. Lindbergh

Disillusioned Europe and speakeasy America got a cool, clean, breath of inspiration from a drama played out by a young man alone over the Atlantic. The date: May 20, 1927. That morning, at Roosevelt Field on Long Island, a slim, lanky figure climbed into the cockpit of a light, silver-painted airplane. At 7:52, the plane was airborne. On its wings soared the hopes and aspirations of a soul-sick world, for this was the Lone Eagle, Charles A. Lindbergh, who overnight became the greatest hero of his time. When The Spirit of St. Louis touched down in Paris, the world had found the romantic figure it so desperately craved.

The age of powered flight had begun a quarter of a century earlier when, on Dec. 17, 1903, at Kitty Hawk, N.C., two brothers, Orville and Wilbur Wright, after years of experimentation, made four successful flights with a 750-pound, 12 horsepower airplane. Length of the first flight: 120 feet.

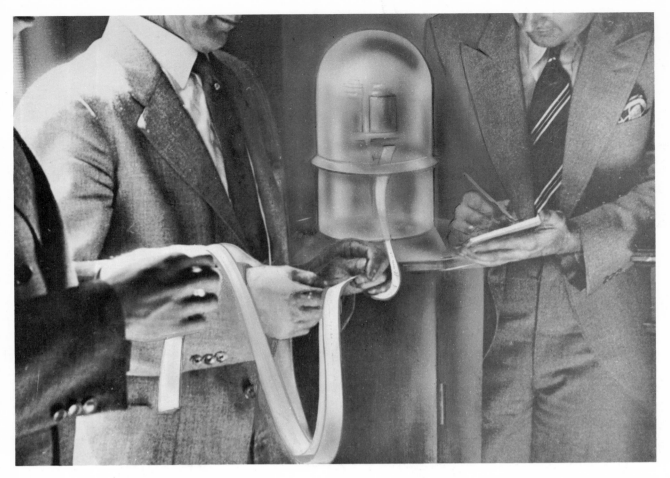

Watching the ticker tape; the paper band carrying the latest stock quotations symbolized the great bull market

President Herbert Hoover reads inaugural speech

During the ebullient days of the Coolidge Administration, stock prices climbed upward in the greatest bull market of all time. By 1927, the price of stocks had become purely speculative. America was on a gambling spree, but as astronomically inflated as it was, the market received another dizzying boost with the election of Herbert Hoover in 1928. "We in America today," declared Hoover, "are nearer to the final triumph over poverty than ever before in the history of any land." And so, most certainly, it seemed. Responding volatilely, the bull market soared to its final, fantastic heights in the summer of 1929. During an 18-month period, the stock of U.S. Steel and Union Carbide doubled in price, Montgomery Ward tripled, RCA quintupled. On slender margin (only 10 per cent of the purchase price had to be in cash), the gambling grew reckless. Intoxicated by the rising market, the nation seemed oblivious to the storm clouds gathering at home and abroad.

Defying *the League, the Japanese marched into Manchuria, the first step in their master plan to conquer Asia*

The march on Rome *behind him, Mussolini hatched grandiose schemes of Mediterranean domination, African conquest*

Chaos in Germany, *and waiting in the wings, Adolf Hitler*

Power-Mad Men

The signs were there to see, but as the gay frenetic decade slipped away, a self-indulgent America was in no mood to read the portents of disaster. Already Benito Mussolini had marched on Rome at the head of his black-shirted rabble, consolidated his political power and emerged as Il Duce; in Germany, the strident voice of the power-mad ex-corporal, Adolf Hitler, could be heard screaming of a pure Germany for pure Germans, the master race which had been betrayed in the war by Jewish businessmen, Jewish bankers; and in the Far East, militarists in Tokyo were planning their first step for Asian conquest.

'American Farm,' *in this stark allegory, artist Joe Jones depicts an American farm ravaged by erosion and dust storms .*

. the painting symbolized in harsh detail the farmer's plight

THE DUST BOWL
IN THE 1930's

Scale of Miles

© C. S. Hammond & Co.

Most of America's economy prospered mightily during the '20s, but the farmer sank deeper into a secular depression of his own. Pressed by demands to feed a hungry world in World War I, with new machinery and new techniques, the farmer was now producing far more than the nation could consume. Millions of acres of land had been brought into production. Farm prices, therefore, dropped drastically, but the farmer's expenses did not. The problem of farm surpluses was to trouble agricultural experts, economists, and legislators for years to come. Legislation was developed to protect the farmer against market exploitation, to foster cooperative marketing, and to give them easier access to credit. But their lot failed to improve. This faulty balance between agriculture and the rest of the economy was a grim portent as the decade drew to a close. Other danger signs in the economy were epidemic-like speculation in the stock market and real estate, overextension of credit, and abuses in the banking system. But overuse of the land—the rampant production for war needs—was already bringing the first gritty warning of a blight to fall on millions of acres of farm land and on thousands of farm families—the dust storms.

On Black Tuesday, Wall Street was a scene of panic as thousands of brokers and investors milled about after the crash

Apples, the symbol of the depression

This Was Black Tuesday . .

After fluctuating erratically during September 1929, the market began an ominous downhill slide. On Oct. 24, a selling wave broke over the New York Stock Exchange. Then came Tuesday, Oct. 29, 1929, the blackest day in the history of the stock market. On that day, a record 16,410,030 transactions took place. In a few frantic hours prices of major stocks plunged nearly 40 points. Brokers were swamped with sell orders. As surely as the trap-door under a condemned man, the bottom dropped out of the market. In the two weeks that followed, security values shrank by $25 billion. "Wall Street Lays an Egg" was the trade paper *Variety*'s headline. But it was no joke. The financial community was in near panic; suicides were common. And the stock market crash touched off the greatest depression ever known. The party was over.

"I see nothing in the situation which warrants pes-

The smokeless chimneys in the nation's steel mills starkly reminded Americans of hard times at hand, hard times ahead

A British coffee stall had handouts for needy

... The Day the Wheels Stopped

FREE TO THE NEEDY

EE TO THE NEEDY

THE WELCOME

XX 27

simism," declared Secretary of the Treasury Mellon in a hopeful message on New Year's Day 1930. But pessimism had become a virus. An economic collapse of momentous proportions was in the making, its repercussions to be felt everywhere. Industrial production fell off rapidly. New construction virtually ceased. More than 85,000 businesses went under in three years; 5,000 banks failed. Wages were cut drastically; white-collar and blue-collar workers alike suffered. Farmers were particularly hard hit; foreclosures were common. Savings were soon wiped out; millions were in debt. Steel mills banked their fires, bread lines stretched from relief missions, and men sold apples in the streets. The great depression was world-wide. In 1931, Britain was forced to abandon the gold standard, and that great edifice of world finance, built up so carefully for a century, came crashing down.

THE
BONUS OCCUPATION ARMY
IN WASHINGTON, D. C.
1932

After the destruction of their campsites the Bonus Army dispersed to Maryland and Pennsylvania. Lacking effective leadership and organization, the Bonus Army came to an end as members returned home.

Here, on the flats of Anacostia, 10,000 bonus seekers encamped. Tents and shanties served as quarters.

A N A C O S T I A

On the evening of June 28, U. S. troops forced the Bonus Army to evacuate their main camp in Anacostia. Their makeshift quarters were burned and all approaches to the city closed.

The Bonus Army that occupied Washington came from all sections of the country; some arriving on foot, others by car or truck. They numbered about 17,000 ex-servicemen.

Eleventh St.

While Congress deliberated the Patman Bonus Bill thousands of bonus seekers demonstrated in front of the Capitol.

Seventh St.

Third St.

K St.

N. E.

East Capitol St.

B St.

G St.

M St.

S. E.

Pennsylvania Ave.

Fifteenth St.

U. S. NAVY YARD

A N A C O S T I A   R I V E R

LIBRARY OF CONGRESS

UNION STATION

Massachusetts Ave.

North Capitol St.

South Capitol St.

U. S. CAPITOL

Bonus Bill was passed in the House of Representatives but was defeated in the Senate, June 17th. Large numbers of Veterans began the return journey home.

Third St.

N. W.

S. W.

On July 28 violence broke out between the Bonus Army and District Police. Two men were killed and a number injured. District officials requested Federal troops to restore order.

Several hundred Bonus Army men were driven from quarters in semi-demolished buildings by U. S. troops using bayonets and tear gas.

WAR COLLEGE

Pennsylvania Ave.

Constitution Ave.

SMITHSONIAN INSTITUTION

Maryland Ave.

W A S H I N G T O N   C H A N N E L

E

N

S

W

EAST POTOMAC PARK

Route of march for 500 U. S. troops consisting of cavalry, infantry and six light tanks.

Twelfth St.

TREASURY DEPT.

Fifteenth St.

THE WHITE HOUSE

WASHINGTON MONUMENT

Seventeenth St.

STATE, WAR AND NAVY DEPARTMENTS

Staging area for U. S. troops ordered out by President Hoover and commanded by Gen. Douglas MacArthur.

TIDAL BASIN

POTOMAC RIVER

Scale in Feet

0   1000   2000   3000   4000

© C. S. Hammond & Co.

This painting, 'Employment Agency,' by Isaac Soyer depicted a scene familiar in many countries during the great depression

By 1932, the depression had deepened and broadened: More than 10 million Americans were unemployed. To cope with the disaster, the President organized conferences and issued cheerful statements, while his critics insisted more drastic Federal action was needed. Among the President's problems was the "Bonus Army," a band of World War I veterans, 10,000 strong, who marched to Washington and encamped there in shabby hovels, hoping to bring pressure on Congress to vote them funds. After a clash between the vets and local police, Hoover called out the Army. Leading infantry, cavalry and tanks, Gen. Douglas MacArthur, Chief of Staff, routed the bonus army and burned their shacks. Thus, the Wilsonian ideals that marked American participation in World War I were dragged through the mud flats of Washington.

In shacks like these, depression's squatters lived

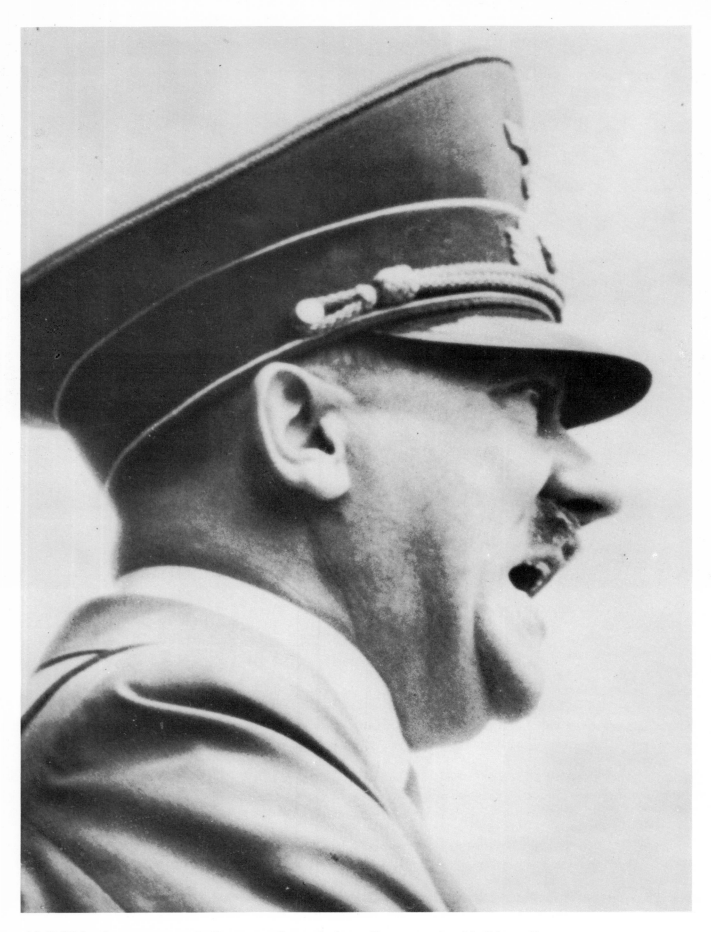

Adolf Hitler *harangues a typically rapt audience during a German national holiday rally*

"This wicked man Hitler, the repository and embodiment of many forms of soul-destroying hatred, this monstrous product of former wrongs and shame."

Winston Churchill, 1940

The World of Dictators

Wandering helplessly in the political and economic rubble of post World War I Europe, nation after nation fell into the iron grip of the strong man—the Dictator. In Italy, Mussolini came into power; in Russia, Lenin, then Stalin; in Spain, Franco. But it was in Germany that the world was to witness the rise of the most terrible dictator of all time, a tyrant without match in the whole sorry history of inhumanity—Adolf Hitler.

Born in Austria the son of a petty official, Adolf Hitler was a shiftless drifter until he enlisted in the German Army in World War I. After Germany's defeat, there followed for Hitler "terrible days and even worse nights . . . My hatred arose against the originators of this deed." In 1919 Hitler joined a small political group soon to be known as the National Socialist German Workers party, or "Nazi" for short; in 1921 he became Der Fuehrer—the leader.

As the Weimar Republic faltered during the turbulent years of the 1920s, the Nazi Party gathered momentum. To his followers—and to all Germans—Hitler promised to restore the nation's power, wealth, and glory. As a demagogue, Hitler became a genius. He had a sure, instinctive grasp of the mass psychology of his countrymen; and his shrill, near-hysterical speeches were singularly effective in releasing the well-springs of his audiences' emotions—the passion, hatred, and fury of the mob. To those audiences, Hitler was a messiah who would deliver them from bondage and redress all wrongs.

By any ordinary standards, Adolf Hitler was insane. Yet he came close to destroying a civilization that was thousands of years in the building; and it would take the combined military might of America, the British Commonwealth, the Soviet Union and France to bring down his monstrous creation, the Third Reich. But from 1933 to 1945, Hitler was Der Fuehrer to Germany and mighty nations trembled as he gobbled up territory and marched inexorably to World War II.

The World in Ferment

GREENLAND

ICELAND

NOR[W]

CANADA

UNITED STATES

Economic Depression

World Wide Economic Trouble

MEXICO

CUBA

HAITI

DOMINICAN REPUBLIC

CENTRAL AMERICA

VENEZUELA

BRITISH GUIANA

DUTCH GUIANA

FRENCH GUIANA

COLOMBIA

ECUADOR

PACIFIC OCEAN

PERU

BRAZIL

BOLIVIA

Chaco War

CHILE

PARAGUAY

ARGENTINA

URUGUAY

Eckert Projection

ATLANTIC OCEAN

IRELAND

GREAT BRITAIN

GERMANY

FRANCE

ITALY

PORTUGAL

SPAIN

TUNISIA

MOROCCO

ALGERIA

LIB[Y]

RIO DE ORO

FRENCH WEST AFRICA

GAMBIA

PORT. GUINEA

SIERRA LEONE

LIBERIA

GOLD COAST

TOGO

NIGERIA

CAMERO[ON]

FR[

World Trade Decline

ANG[OLA]

SOUTH-WEST AFRICA

To a world barely recovering from the shattering effects of World War I, the depression came as a staggering setback. The repercussions, complex and inter-related, were felt everywhere—from breadlines in Illinois to famine in the Ukraine. Ships rusted at anchor. The normal arteries of trade between nations withered. Unrest spread. With capitalism in disgrace, totalitarian systems gained in strength. Mussolini glanced covetously beyond the Mediterranean; Hitler talked ominously of more "living room" for Ger-

mans. The world was torn by strife. Latin America wallowed in wars and revolutions. Led by Gandhi, Indians rose against the British rulers. The Chinese Communists began their long war of attrition against Chiang Kai-shek's Nationalists. Under control of an arrogant military dictatorship, Japan occupied all of Manchuria and dispatched planes to bomb helpless Shanghai. The League of Nations remained impotent; America, Britain, and France retained smug postures of pacifism as the world neared the holocaust.

Roehm, *the Storm Troop boss purged by Hitler*

In Germany, Hitler was surrounding himself with his vicious henchmen, the men Winston Churchill called "the grisly gang who work your wicked will." The influential members of the Nazi party were indeed a ghastly crew: Hermann Goering, Hitler's chief deputy, a World War I aviator turned Sybarite who would command the feared Luftwaffe; Rudolf Hess, the erratic party strategist; Heinrich Himmler, the ruthless boss of the Gestapo; Ernst Roehm, the aberrant Storm Trooper whom Hitler later ordered murdered; Joseph Paul Goebbels, the evil genius of propaganda; and Julius Streicher, who led the unbelievably scurrilous condemnation of Hitler's scapegoats: The Jews.

Goering: *No. 2 Nazi*

Streicher, *Hitler's anti-Semitic merchant of hate*

Hitler with Goebbels: *From a brilliant mind, evil propaganda*

A **Jewish lawyer** who complained about Nazi terror is forced to recant

Storm Troopers drag another Jew through the streets in a junk wagon

Nazi vandals desecrated Jewish gravestones in this Rhineland cemetery

Though Hitler blamed Germany's ills on everything from the Versailles Treaty to Communist subversion, in his bitterest attacks, he singled out the Jews. "In a people like the German people," he observed, "it is absolutely necessary for psychological reasons to point to only one enemy, to march against one enemy." At first, Jews were forbidden to hold public office and limited in choice of careers; later, they were deprived of citizenship. As anti-Semitism spread, Jews were mobbed by Storm Troopers, shops were looted, synagogues burned. Such acts were an outrage, but as the world was soon to see, only a faint prelude of the horrors yet to come.

These Were the Roots of Hitler's Reich

With conditions as they were in post-war Germany, the Weimar Republic was in trouble from the very beginning. At no time did any of the political parties hold a majority in Parliament, the Reichstag; thus the government was never really strong, or even popular. Hitler's National Socialism, on the other hand, provided a banner behind which the disillusioned and the discontented could rally—the lower-middle class suffering from inflation; unemployed veterans; German youth eager for patriotic causes; the Army seeking to regain lost status; industrialists foreseeing fat profits in rearmament; businessmen fearing the rise of Communism; and the plain millions who resented occupation troops and reparations payments. In 1923 in Munich, Hitler attempted to seize power in the abortive beer-hall putsch but was thrown in jail, where he wrote *Mein Kampf* ("My Struggle"). Few took the Nazis seriously in the middle 1920s, but the party flourished; and with the advent of the depression, National Socialism became the major force in German politics. President Hindenburg was forced to recognize Hitler's popular support; and on Jan. 30, 1933, the aging ex-Field Marshal appointed the young ex-corporal Chancellor. That act marked the end of the Weimar Republic and the beginning of the Third Reich.

In this brooding painting, aging President Hindenburg hands the baton of power to the new German Chancellor, Adolf Hitler

The Reichstag with its dedication 'To the German People' was a proud symbol of Parliamentary government . . .

. . . and its destruction by flames symbolized the rise of Hitlerism

One month after Hitler became Chancellor—just six days before the national election—the Reichstag building, seat of Parliament in Berlin, went up in flames. Who destroyed the Reichstag? "The Communists," trumpeted the Nazis, and jailed hundreds of left-wing party members. The responsibility for the fire was never cleared up though there was little doubt that the plot grew in the fertile minds of Dr. Joseph Goebbels and Hermann Goering. But the incident gave the Nazis the excuse they needed to incite hysteria against their political foes. On election day, Hitler's National Socialists got 44 per cent of the vote. The near-majority was the signal for Hitler's private army, the Storm Troopers, to arrest thousands of Communists, Socialists and Jews. They also jailed newly-elected Communist deputies — thereby giving the Nazis a clear majority in the Reichstag. With this violent flourish, Hitler then quickly had the Reichstag pass an "Enabling Act" granting him absolute power for four years—and he outlawed all political parties except the Nazis. Hitler was now master of the Third Reich, free to carry out his "New Order."

itler's New Order cut deep into German life. At all levels, and by all means, the people were to be indoctrinated, and inspired by Joseph Goebbels' masterfully adroit propaganda. In schools the teachers preached courage in battle, obedience, and unswerving belief in the superiority of the Aryan race. When knowledge did not serve the ends of the Nazi cause, it was quickly dispensed with; books considered offensive were denounced and banned, or burned in great bonfires. The duty of the student was not to think, said Der Fuehrer, but to obey. Boys and girls were regimented in Hitler's youth organizations where they learned to drill and handle weapons. In this Spartan regime, the family was superseded by the state as the social unit; mothers became brood mares. All forms of communication, even the arts, became instruments of propaganda devoted to the glorification of Hitler and the vilification of the Jews. And, in violation of the Versailles Treaty, Germany rearmed and prepared for war.

Members of Hitler's Youth *gleefully burned books in a Salzburg square*

Trained on gliders, *these pilots would soon man the Luftwaffe's planes*

In speech after speech, Der Fuehrer instilled into Germany the doctrine of the Master Race. At mass meetings (photo, opposite page), millions of Germans took an oath: "We again bind ourselves to a man through whom . . . superior forces act in fulfillment of Destiny. Do not seek Adolf Hitler with your brains; you will find him with the strength of your hearts. Adolf Hitler is Germany and Germany is Adolf Hitler." To the multitudes, Hitler began to speak menacingly of "Lebensraum," living space for the Reich, and of righting the injustices inflicted at Versailles. "Only the might of a triumphal sword," Hitler had warned in *Mein Kampf*, "will in the future assign us territory, and with it life for our nation." The words were there for the world to hear; but the world paid scant attention.

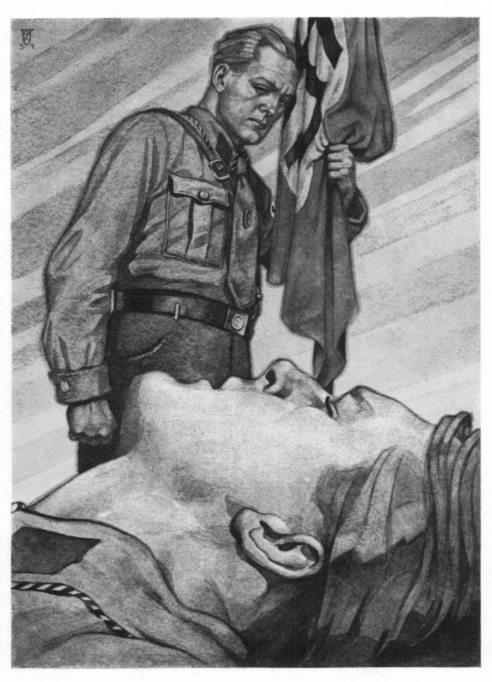

In this propaganda poster, *a young Nazi vows to a fallen comrade to carry on for Der Fuehrer*

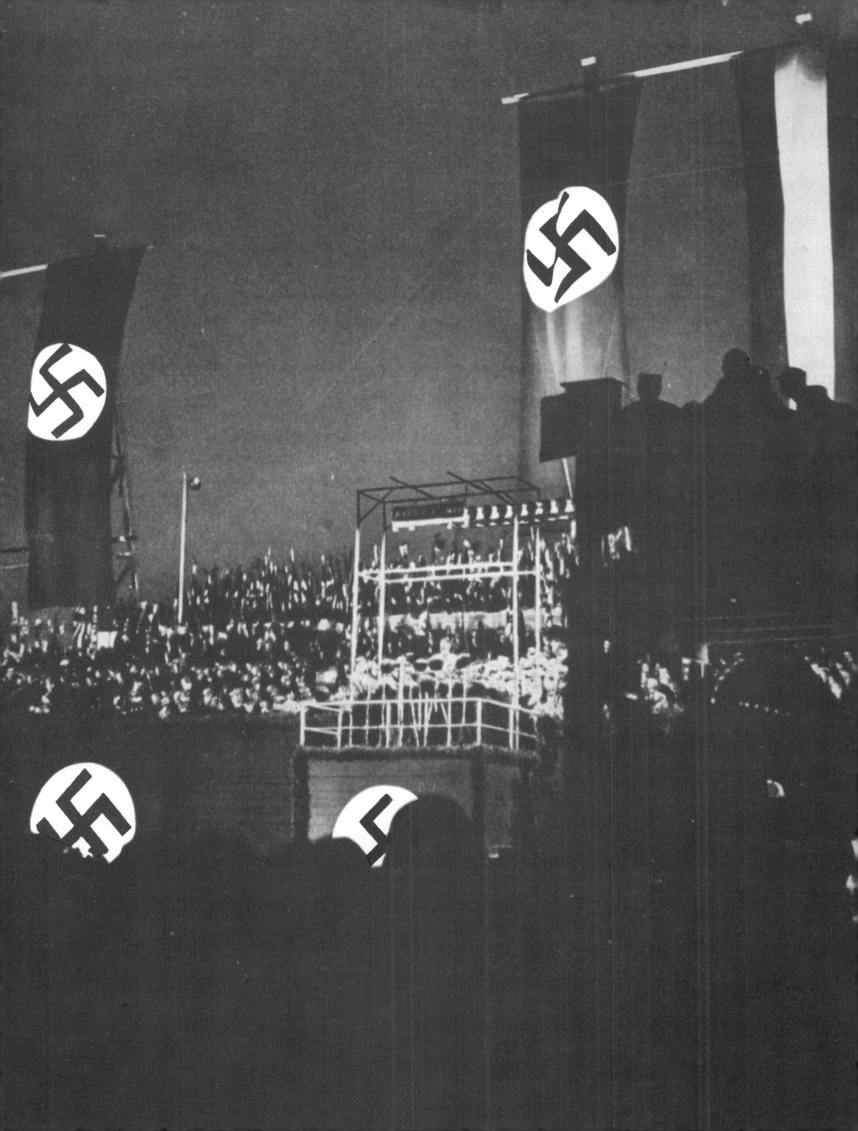

Cheering throngs greet a German regiment occupying a Rhineland town

By 1935, Nazi Germany was a power to reckon with. In January, the rich Saar Valley (separated from Germany by the Versailles Treaty) voted to reunite with the Third Reich; in March, Hitler revived the air force and restored universal compulsory military service. In June, he repudiated the naval construction provisions of the Versailles Treaty in return for a promise to Britain to limit his naval tonnage to 35 per cent of England's—a move which would give Germany a fleet rivaling France's. But Hitler's greatest triumph was yet to come: On March 7, 1936, German soldiers entered the demilitarized Rhineland—in clear violation of the Versailles Treaty. It was a stunning gamble. France could easily have driven Hitler back to Germany. But Hitler shrewdly guessed that Europe was too preoccupied or too timid to interfere. France hesitated; Britain vacillated; and the precious opportunity to cut Hitler down to size was forever lost. The world would pay with millions of lives for failing to stop Hitler when it could. And through the streets of the Rhineland rang the words of the Nazis' marching song: "Today Germany is ours; tomorrow the world."

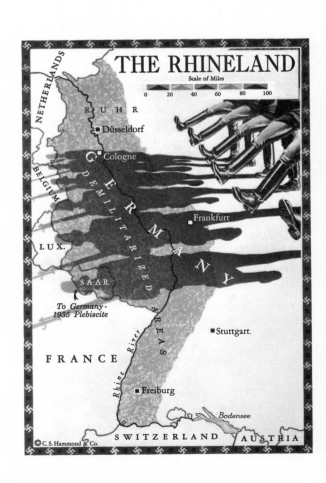

Now Hitler armed in earnest, *and the German Army became the most skilled and most efficient striking force in modern times*

Down the ways *slid the hulls of new warships*

In constant maneuvers, *the quick-striking Wehrmacht emerged*

The artillery *was well supplied by Ruhr steel*

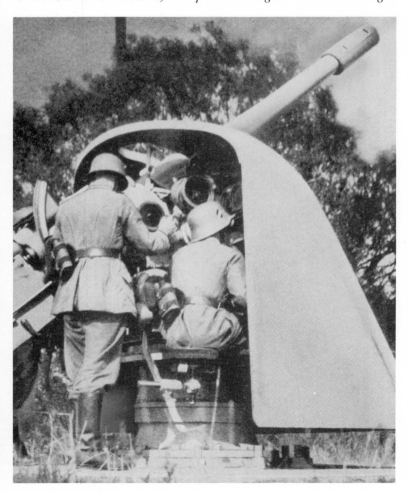

135

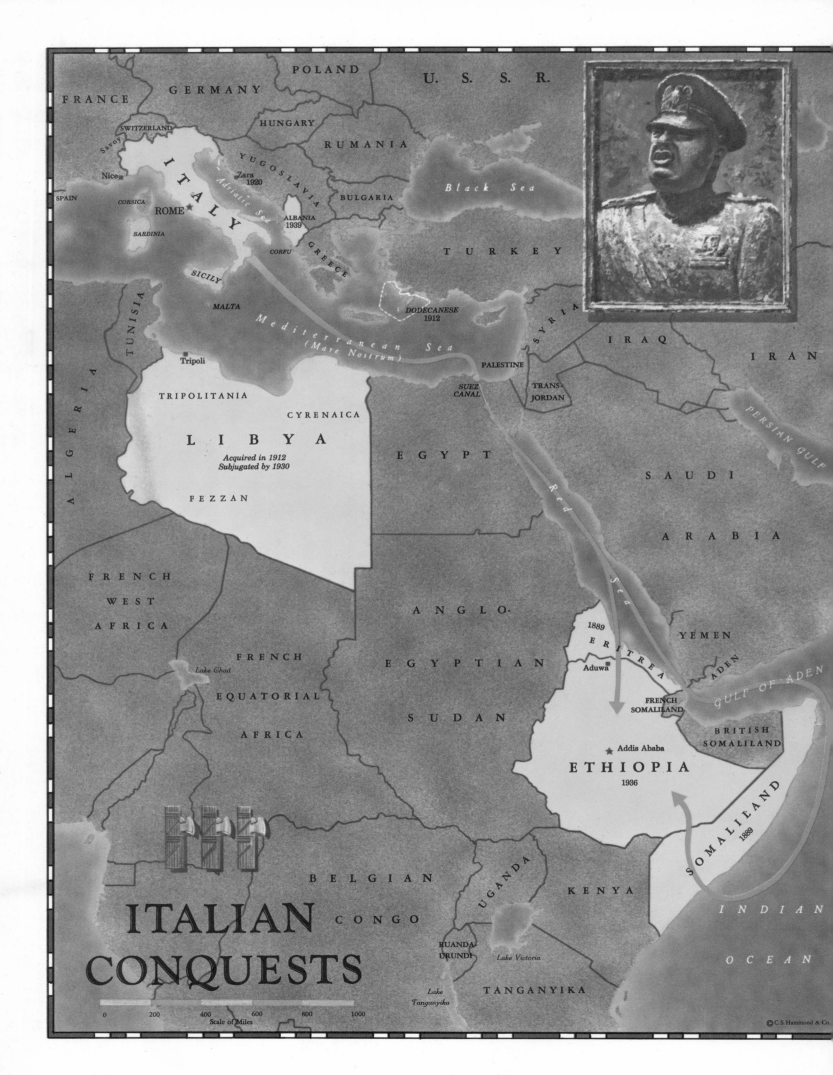

FRANCE
GERMANY
POLAND
U. S. S. R.
SWITZERLAND
HUNGARY
Savoy
RUMANIA
Nice
Zara
1920
ITALY
Adriatic Sea
Black Sea
SPAIN
CORSICA
YUGOSLAVIA
ALBANIA
1939
ROME
SARDINIA
CORFU
GREECE
TURKEY
SICILY
MALTA
DODECANESE
1912
ALGERIA
TUNISIA
Mediterranean Sea
(Mare Nostrum)
SYRIA
IRAQ
IRAN
Tripoli
PALESTINE
SUEZ
CANAL
TRANS-
JORDAN
PERSIAN GULF
TRIPOLITANIA
CYRENAICA
L I B Y A
EGYPT
Acquired in 1912
Subjugated by 1930
SAUDI
FEZZAN
A R A B I A
Red Sea
FRENCH
WEST
AFRICA
ANGLO-
1889
YEMEN
ERITREA
Aduwa
ADEN
FRENCH
SOMALILAND
GULF OF ADEN
Lake Chad
FRENCH
EGYPTIAN
BRITISH
SOMALILAND
EQUATORIAL
SUDAN
Addis Ababa
AFRICA
ETHIOPIA
1936
SOMALILAND
1889

ITALIAN

BELGIAN
CONGO
UGANDA
KENYA
INDIAN

CONQUESTS

RUANDA-
URUNDI
Lake Victoria
OCEAN
Lake
Tanganyika
TANGANYIKA

0   200   400   600   800   1000
Scale of Miles

©C.S.Hammond & Co.

The Dictator in Rome

In Rome, another dictator—Benito Mussolini—saw in Hitler's successful defiance of Versailles the guidepost for his own march to conquest. Italy, which had long resented British and French ascendancy in Africa, gazed covetously at one unplucked plum. Lying between Italian Somaliland and Eritrea was Ethiopia, ruled by the King of Kings, Emperor Haile Selassie. "The Italian character must be formed through fighting," decreed Il Duce. Backward Ethiopia, nearly defenseless, would be the means. Once before, in 1896, an Italian army had invaded Ethiopia only to suffer humiliating defeat. Now, under Marshal Pietro Badoglio, the Italian forces, equipped with the latest weapons, airplanes, and poison gas, marched against Haile Selassie's primitive army.

Marshal Pietro Badoglio *led the Italian assault against Ethiopia*

Selassie fought back, *but Mussolini finally won*

137

At the League of Nations, after economic sanctions proved ineffectual, Emperor Haile Selassie spoke with moving eloquence

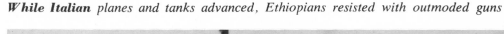

While Italian planes and tanks advanced, Ethiopians resisted with outmoded guns

Only one force could save Ethiopia: The League of Nations. Once before, when Japan marched into Manchuria, the League had failed to stop an aggressor. Publicly, both France and Britain endorsed the League, but neither was ready to step on Mussolini's toes. They hoped that Il Duce would side with them against the rising German menace. After long procrastination, the League did vote economic sanctions against Italy, but they were ineffective and only succeeded in driving a bitter Mussolini closer to the Nazi camp. Badoglio pressed relentlessly forward, and Selassie made a final appeal to the conscience of the world: "I pray to Almighty God that he may spare nations the terrible sufferings which have just been inflicted on my people." The League turned away the Emperor's plea. Again an aggressor had gone unpunished.

General Franco *gives the Fascist salute as he reviews his Moorish troops, the backbone of his rebel Army*

'War Game' in Prostrate Spain

It was inevitable that Fascism and Communism—the evil ideologies grown from the ashes of World War I—would come into direct conflict on the battlefield. Spain was the unhappy land to endure the first taste of "modern" warfare. In 1936, the Spanish Popular Front won a substantial victory in the national election, but, behind the scenes, opposition forces—the Army, the church, the elite—plotted a return to power. Urged on by secret promises of aid from Hitler and Mussolini, Fascist General Francisco Franco took command of 55,000 Moorish troops and foreign legionnaires, seized control of Spanish Morocco, and called on mainland garrisons to join him in his revolution. When virtually the whole Army heeded his call, it seemed the Civil War would be over almost before it started. But the Loyalist government found sympathy abroad—and a powerful ally: Communist Russia. Civil War erupted—and tore deep wounds into prostrate Spain, but it was only a dress rehearsal of the greater war to come.

New York Governor Franklin Roosevelt defeated Herbert Hoover , took office in March 1933

The Roosevelt Age

As cannons thundered elsewhere, America sought a way out of the depression. To lead this massive effort, the nation turned in 1932 to neither a radical proletarian nor a militant nationalist, but, instead, to a landed aristocrat —Franklin Delano Roosevelt, who pledged "a new deal for the American people." Though he was no dedicated theorist, Roosevelt was to change the whole concept of government's role with such welfare agencies as the Works Progress Administration. And a dispirited nation rallied behind his words: "The only thing we have to fear is fear itself."

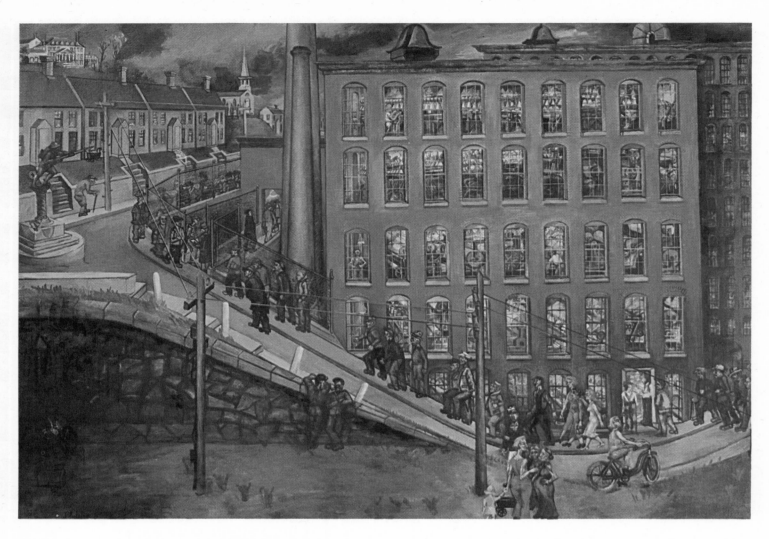

*'**Through the Mill**' by Philip Evergood depicted the first murmurings of American industrial recovery*

Once in office, President Roosevelt moved quickly in his program of relief, recovery, and reform. To give financial institutions a breathing spell, F.D.R. declared a bank holiday. Then Congress, in the first "hundred days of Roosevelt" passed a great mass of legislation. In those months, and in the years that followed, came such "alphabet" measures as the Civilian Conservation Corps (CCC), the Agricultural Adjustment Administration (AAA), the National Recovery Administration (NRA), the WPA, the Public Works Administration (PWA), the Rural Electrification Administration (REA), the Federal Housing Administration (FHA), the Tennessee Valley Authority (TVA), and that cornerstone of the New Deal, the Social Security Act. Congress also strengthened government's power to regulate business with the Securities and Exchange Commission, the

Federal Deposit Insurance Corporation, and the Federal Communications Commission. With the creation of these agencies, a revolution had occurred: Government had fully departed from the tradition that the "least governed are the best governed"—instead, government played an active, social-service role in affairs—and was alternately praised and damned for it. As political weight shifted from the upper and middle class to the lower-middle class and the workers, an "explosion" of trade unionism was set off. The National Labor Relations Act established the right of workers to organize and bargain collectively, and in the middle '30s, the nation was harried by a series of strikes. Sometimes the walkouts grew into massive violence—to the dismay of the nation. Of the notorious Republic Steel-CIO conflict President Roosevelt himself declared: "A plague on both your houses."

An American tragedy, the bloody clash between police and strikers at Republic Steel in Chicago

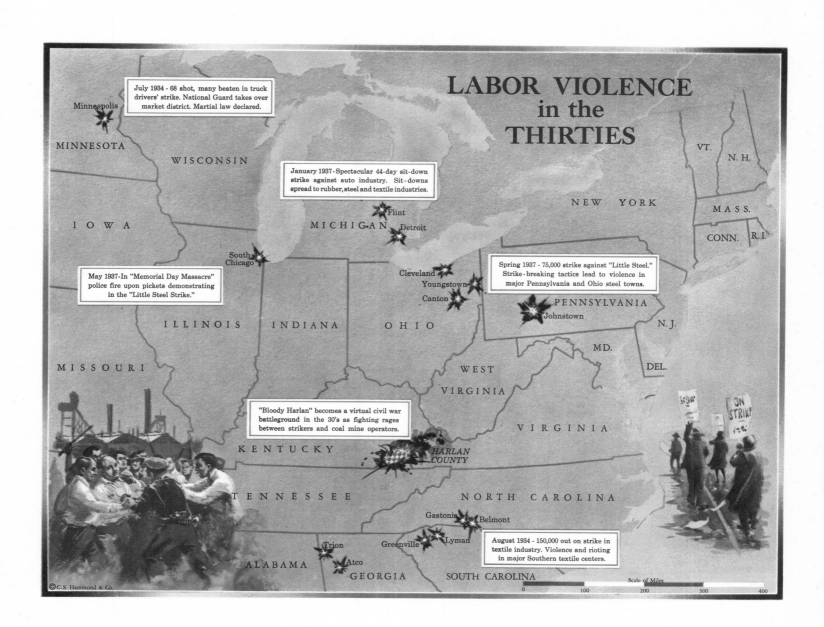

LABOR VIOLENCE in the THIRTIES

July 1934 - 68 shot, many beaten in truck drivers' strike. National Guard takes over market district. Martial law declared.

January 1937 - Spectacular 44-day sit-down strike against auto industry. Sit-downs spread to rubber, steel and textile industries.

May 1937 - In "Memorial Day Massacre" police fire upon pickets demonstrating in the "Little Steel Strike."

Spring 1937 - 75,000 strike against "Little Steel." Strike-breaking tactics lead to violence in major Pennsylvania and Ohio steel towns.

"Bloody Harlan" becomes a virtual civil war battleground in the 30's as fighting rages between strikers and coal mine operators.

August 1934 - 150,000 out on strike in textile industry. Violence and rioting in major Southern textile centers.

© C.S. Hammond & Co.

Scale of Miles
0   100   200   300   400

153

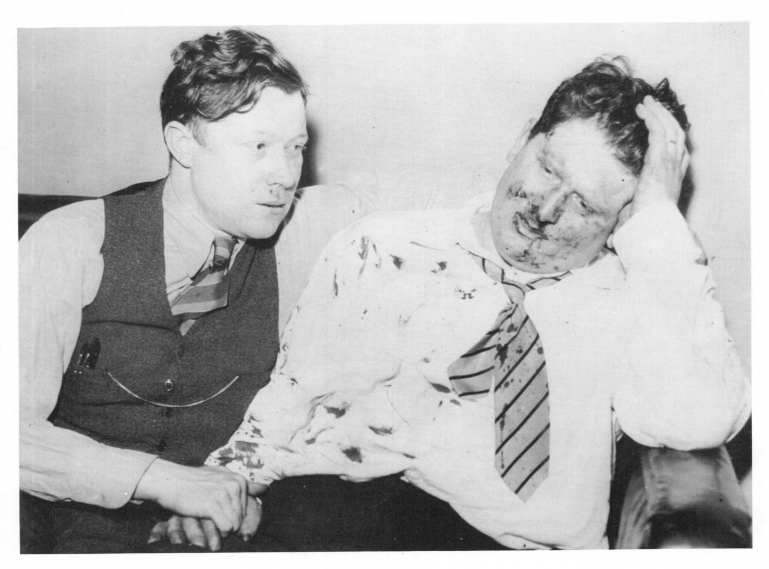

Walter Reuther and Richard Frankensteen of United Automobile Workers were mauled in battle to unionize Ford

In the wave of sit-down strikes, a Flint worker naps

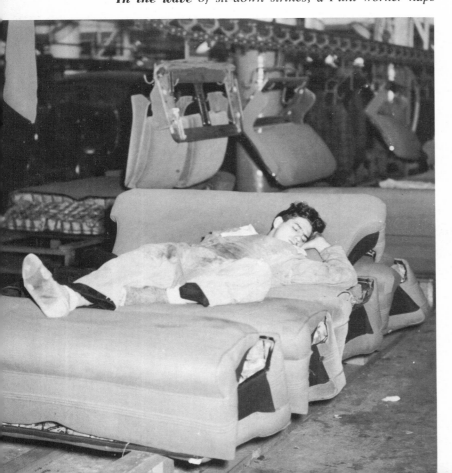

Labor unrest in the '30s brought a new, defiant weapon into labor disputes—the sit-down strike. By the plant-full, employees refused either to work or to leave the building. The sit-down strike was effective, especially in the automobile industry, until ruled illegal. The violence of the times was reflected by the struggles in the unions themselves. The American Federation of Labor, the traditional craft union, found itself challenged from within by those who insisted mass production industries should be organized along industrial lines. This dissension reached a peak at the 1935 convention when John L. Lewis, head of the United Mine Workers', physically knocked down William L. Hutcheson, of the Carpenter's Union; soon after, Lewis founded the rival Congress of Industrial Organizations. Though the two unions fought many a jurisdictional battle, the rivalry spurred organizing efforts. The CIO established itself in the auto, steel, rubber and many other industries, while the AFL also continued to grow. By 1941, labor organizations could claim 11 million members.

Prof. Raymond Moley *led braintrusters to Washington*

In the early days of the New Deal, President Roosevelt brought both professors and politicians to his side in the battle for his new views. There was the famous "braintrust," recruited from the academic community and led by Prof. Raymond Moley of Columbia University. It was a stimulating time in Washington and the intellectuals vied for the Presidential ear with backroom professionals. Though the braintrusters were a frequent target of the conservative press, many were less radical than generally painted; Professor Moley, in fact, parted company with President Roosevelt over policy differences. Others, like Rexford G. Tugwell, and A.A. Berle Jr., remained for years. Perhaps the one scheme of Roosevelt's which caused the most furor during the '30s was his plan to enlarge the Supreme Court. Thoroughly conservative, the Court had handed down a series of decisions adverse to the New Deal. In retaliation, Roosevelt introduced a judicial reform bill to enlarge the court of the "nine old men" to 15 members. The proposed legislation backfired spectacularly; after a long and bitter fight, the Senate killed the bill by a huge margin. The President licked his wounds, but within four years Court vacancies caused by death and retirement gave him the opportunity to appoint seven justices to the Court, thereby assuring a "Roosevelt Court."

The 'nine old men' of the Supreme Court in 1937. Front: Louis D. Brandeis, Willis Van Devanter, Chief Justice Charles Evans Hughes, James C. McReynolds, George Sutherland. Back: Owen J. Roberts, Pierce Butler, Harlan F. Stone, Benjamin N. Cardozo

New York harbor came alive with commerce again as the arrival of ships symbolized an upturn of world trade

After the dark days of 1931-32, the country witnessed a period of economic recovery—whether because of the New Deal, as Democrats claimed; or in spite of it, as Republicans charged. By 1936, the economic situation had, to a degree, improved; national income and industrial production made encouraging gains, and President Roosevelt was able to announce that for the first time in 55 years, a year had gone by without a national bank failure. Meanwhile, Congress passed a reciprocal trade law which authorized the

President to make special agreements with other nations to encourage the resumption of trade; and by the end of the '30s, pacts had been signed with 21 nations accounting for 60 per cent of the nation's foreign commerce. In 1937, however, just as things were looking up, a discouraging setback took place: A recession—caused in part by the deflationary activities of an over-confident administration. But the summer of 1938 saw the downward trend reversed; and by December, much of the lost ground had been regained. And with the huge military preparedness expenditures in the offing, the great depression could be gratefully considered history.

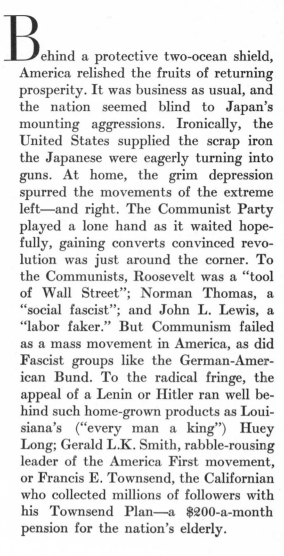

Behind a protective two-ocean shield, America relished the fruits of returning prosperity. It was business as usual, and the nation seemed blind to Japan's mounting aggressions. Ironically, the United States supplied the scrap iron the Japanese were eagerly turning into guns. At home, the grim depression spurred the movements of the extreme left—and right. The Communist Party played a lone hand as it waited hopefully, gaining converts convinced revolution was just around the corner. To the Communists, Roosevelt was a "tool of Wall Street"; Norman Thomas, a "social fascist"; and John L. Lewis, a "labor faker." But Communism failed as a mass movement in America, as did Fascist groups like the German-American Bund. To the radical fringe, the appeal of a Lenin or Hitler ran well behind such home-grown products as Louisiana's ("every man a king") Huey Long; Gerald L.K. Smith, rabble-rousing leader of the America First movement, or Francis E. Townsend, the Californian who collected millions of followers with his Townsend Plan—a $200-a-month pension for the nation's elderly.

Girders of New York's elevated opposite Radio City, were torn down for scrap

Huge piles of scrap metal were loaded aboard freighters bound for Japan's mills

Not Hitler Youth — *young Bund members in America*

American girls *also marched at Nazi Camp Nordland, N.J.*

In New York, *2,500 Communists demonstrated at the German consulate*

Earl Browder, *American Red leader*

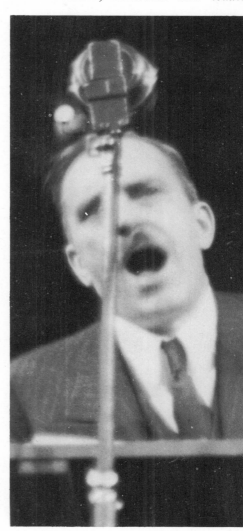

159

Little Shirley Temple reigned during the '30s

Ás money began to flow again, the nation devoted more and more time to entertainment, and to idol-worship. Among the big names in sports were baseball's Dizzy Dean, track's Jesse Owens, boxing's Joe Louis, and the Triple Crown racing winners—Gallant Fox, Omaha, and War Admiral. Americans learned a new dance rhythm called "swing" from its chief exponents, Benny Goodman and Tommy Dorsey. But the country's principal diversion was the movie. It was the decade of "bank nite," Walt Disney, Shirley Temple, Mickey Rooney, and the musicals of Ginger Rogers and Fred Astaire. The biggest hit of them all was "Gone With the Wind," adapted from Margaret Mitchell's Civil War novel. The comic book flourished but so did such serious writers as Ernest Hemingway, John Dos Passos, Thomas Wolfe, John Steinbeck, and William Faulkner. Industry forged ahead, particularly aviation. In science, great fundamental discoveries were made as man penetrated the awesome secrets of the atom.

Millions of moviegoers paid to hear the crooner

160

'Gone with the Wind,' *with the English actress Vivien Leigh as Scarlett O'Hara, was a movie sensation . . .*

. . . which starred Clark Gable, 'The King of Hollywood,' in the role of Rhett Butler

F.D.R., *with New York's Governor Lehman (center) and Senator Wagner in the 1936 campaign*

The U.S.S. Langley, *the first American aircraft carrier*

In accepting the Democratic nomination of 1936, President Roosevelt with keen foresight told his listeners: "To some generations much is given. Of other generations much is expected. This generation of Americans has a rendezvous with destiny." Then F.D.R. decided to stand fast with the domestic gains of his first term and devote the larger share of his attention to foreign policy. In his early years in office, the President had tried to improve world accord through international conferences—to little avail. The President faced a serious dilemma: Americans since Wilson's time wanted to remain aloof from foreign alliances, let alone wars; yet the more responsible among them were deeply alarmed by Fascist aggression. The American government thus vigorously deplored aggressive acts; but its indignation was limited to diplomatic rebukes. Even had the government wished to challenge an aggressor, there was little it could do: The American Army was hopelessly out-of-date. Though a few far-sighted officers like Billy Mitchell, Adna R. Chaffee, and George S. Patton Jr., urged development of the air and armored branches, the Army's planes and tanks were antiquated. But finally, in 1938, Congress appropriated the funds to build up defenses, modernize field equipment, increase the enlisted reserve—and construct a two-ocean navy. At last, the nation was rousing herself from 20 years of lethargy in world affairs, a near-coma that almost proved fatal.

In the late '30s the U.S. Army still relied on the horse-drawn artillery of the cavalry—shown here in 'war games'

A tiny, lightly-armed tank, no match for Hitler's armor

Even taxicabs had to be used to transport troops on maneuvers

INSTRUMENT OF ABDICATION

    I, Edward the Eighth, of Great
Britain, Ireland, and the British Dominions
beyond the Seas, King, Emperor of India, do
hereby declare My irrevocable determination
to renounce the Throne for Myself and for
My descendants, and My desire that effect
should be given to this Instrument of
Abdication immediately.

    In token whereof I have hereunto set
My hand this tenth day of December, nineteen
hundred and thirty six, in the presence of
the witnesses whose signatures are subscribed.

SIGNED AT
FORT BELVEDERE
IN THE PRESENCE
OF

With these few words, *a king renounced the throne*   **In a moving speech,** *Edward told his people of his lonely decision*

As Duke of Windsor, *the ex-king married the woman he loved, the American-born Wallis Warfield Simpson*

A King Uncrowned and England Slept

This was a breathless moment. Voluntarily, a king stepped down from the British throne with these simple, dramatic words: "I have found it impossible to carry the heavy burden of responsibility, to discharge my duties as King . . . without the help and support of the woman I love." So His Majesty, King Edward VIII, ended the greatest crisis the empire's monarchy had undergone in modern times.

Edward had rebelled against the orthodoxy of the royal family. He made his friends among the gay Mayfair Set, and there met American-born divorcée Wallis Warfield Simpson. Edward tried to win the consent of Parliament to marry Mrs. Simpson morganatically, but, with the strong backing of the Church of England, the square-jawed, stodgy Prime Minister, Stanley Baldwin, took a firm stand against the match. Romanticists the world over watched the test of strength between the young King and his chief minister. Edward lost and finally abdicated in favor of his younger brother who became George VI. The new King, though afflicted with a serious speech defect, had inherited many of his father's qualities, including a stern sense of duty which would help rally his people in the dark days ahead.

The new King, *George VI, with Queen Elizabeth and daughters Elizabeth and Margaret*

King Edward had departed and Stanley Baldwin was soon to follow. The new Prime Minister, Neville Chamberlain, an earnest man but outwardly as stodgy as Baldwin, was not long in committing himself to a policy of buying peace from the dictators. "Appeasement" was not then an ugly word. His policy reflected the mood of the people. In some sections of England, the dictators were considered guardians of law, order, and private property. To these, the real menace was Communism. Privately, some even hoped that Hitler would subdue Soviet Russia. On the left there were strong groups too, and though the majority rejected both left and right, a discordant chorus arose in England.

Well over a million were unemployed; economic recovery was slow in coming. What, these people asked, had been gained in winning World War I? What would be gained in winning —or losing—another war against the dictators? Students of the Oxford Union, which had provided generations of British leaders, now voted for a resolution: "That this House refuses to fight for King and Country."

A King who abdicated his throne, a nation's youth refusing to fight for its country, a Prime Minister seemingly bent on peace at nearly any price—that was England of the moment. One voice arose to warn of tragedy ahead. Standing in the House of Commons, Winston Churchill told his colleagues: "Do not forget that all the time those remorseless hammers of which General Goering spoke are descending night and day in Germany, and that the most warlike people in Europe are becoming a tremendous fighting machine."

Chamberlain tried to appease the dictators

Winston Churchill foresaw the folly of the Chamberlain policy, warned an unheeding nation of the Hitler menace

British air fleet, *outmoded and understrength*

A sporty *British sergeant heads for overseas duty*

Light battle cruisers *on combined maneuvers*

A fashionable lady *arrives at an Eton-Harrow cricket match*

167

In his dealings with the dictators, Neville Chamberlain was leading from weakness. Britain was in no position to risk a major war. Committed to disarmament among the great powers, previous ministries actually cut military appropriations. The Nazis now possessed more planes, more modern and destructive. What tanks the British had were obsolete. Churchill said it again: "The army lacks every weapon required for modern war." And this under-equipped army was spread around the globe, less than a third of its troops immediately available in Europe. For sea warfare, Germany was building the huge submarine fleet which would go far towards nullifying the apparent British naval superiority. Finally, in 1937, England began a military build-up, but even then it did not match the Nazi effort. In the arms race, Britain fell farther and farther behind.

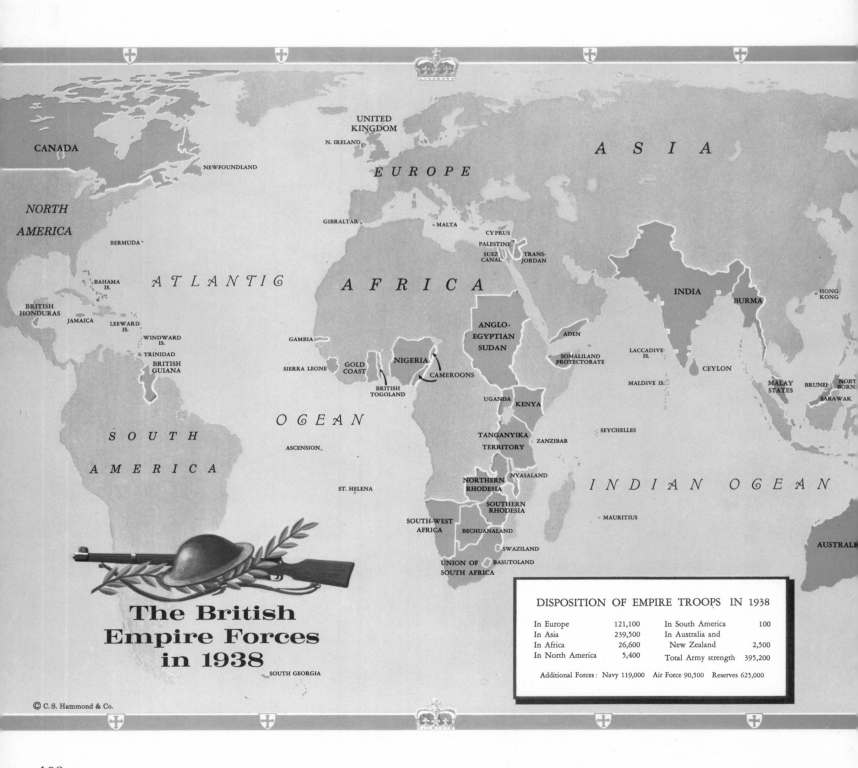

The British Empire Forces in 1938

© C. S. Hammond & Co.

DISPOSITION OF EMPIRE TROOPS IN 1938			
In Europe	121,100	In South America	100
In Asia	239,500	In Australia and	
In Africa	26,600	New Zealand	2,500
In North America	5,400	Total Army strength	395,200
Additional Forces: Navy 119,000		Air Force 90,500	Reserves 625,000

Brilliant colors *capture the atmosphere of gaiety at the Deauville race track in this Raoul Dufy painting*

While a Drifting France Frolicked

Empire-builder Jules Ferry had once said, "What France needs is a weak government." If Ferry had lived into the '30s, he would have had more than he bargained for. At times it seemed there were as many factions as there were Frenchmen, and each of them blind to the gathering clouds of war. Unlike England, in France both the far left and extreme right wielded great power. Governments rose and fell, cabinets constantly reshuffled. And the people themselves drifted aimlessly. Gone was the dedication that in 1914 had halted the Boche at the gates of Paris. At Deauville, in a pre-World War II haze, at Le Touquet, at Biarritz, most Frenchmen put aside any forebodings they may have had for a fling at the races or in the casinos. On the Riviera, party-giving had never been more lavish. At the famed Longchamp racecourse, the advent of night racing produced the greatest traffic jam Paris had ever seen. Leaderless, France was at play.

Lavishly costumed chorus girls kicked their heels high at the Café Bal Tabarin

Frenchmen settled down at sidewalk cafés; the crises made little impression

Even in the world depression, Paris did not lose her charm or her zest. American expatriates who flooded the gay city in the booming '20s packed their bags and returned home, no wiser but poorer, but champagne corks still popped at the Bal Tabarin, Mistinguett showed her $100,000 legs at the Folies Bergère. If these tastes were too rich for the average Frenchman, he still found francs for an aperitif at his favorite café, and he indulged in the national pastime of arguing politics. Politics might be a game to the café-sitter, but the charade was having a deadly effect on France. Using the notorious Stavisky scandals as a pretext (Stavisky, a forger and dealer in worthless securities, had high connections in the cabinet), Fascists marched on the Chamber of Deputies. Revolution was averted, but the fear of rebellion led the parties of the left to form a Popular Front under Socialist Léon Blum. The scholarly, pacifistic Blum, more at home at the literary salon than in rough-and-tumble French politics, was hardly the man to deal with growing crisis. From the beginning, his control of the government was tenuous, resting as it did on the support of 71 Communist deputies. On the right, clandestine Fascist organizations coined a new and ominous slogan: "Better Hitler than Léon Blum."

From flourish to flair, *Paris remained the world's fashion center*

But many *remembered the war that wiped out the youth of France*

France's Blum government embarked on a series of labor reforms. But, as in America, labor responded to this "New Deal" with a wave of sit-down strikes. French production declined 20 per cent while Germany's rose 30 per cent. Much of France's loss of production was at the expense of the military. The German Air Force was growing by 1,000 planes a year while the French stood virtually idle. Over 800,000 Frenchmen might be under arms, the famed academy at St. Cyr might still be turning out young officers (photo, opposite page), but, like the British, the French were not equipped to fight a modern war. France's greatest security lay in the alliances she had built in Eastern Europe which formed a cordon around Nazi Germany. But this advantage would soon go in a wave of appeasement. Germany would break the cordon. As conflict moved ever closer, France, which just a generation before had lost 1.4 million of her young men in battle, had no stomach for another war. Her political system creaking, her national will paralyzed, France seemed bent on suicide.

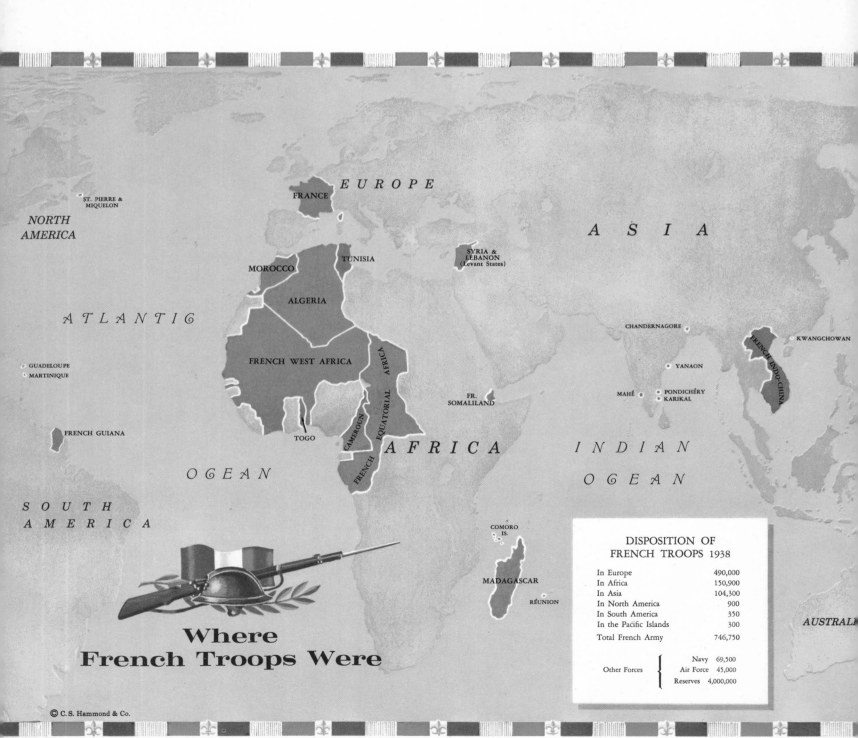

Where French Troops Were

© C.S. Hammond & Co.

DISPOSITION OF FRENCH TROOPS 1938

In Europe	490,000
In Africa	150,900
In Asia	104,300
In North America	900
In South America	350
In the Pacific Islands	300
Total French Army	746,750

Other Forces {	Navy	69,500
	Air Force	45,000
	Reserves	4,000,000

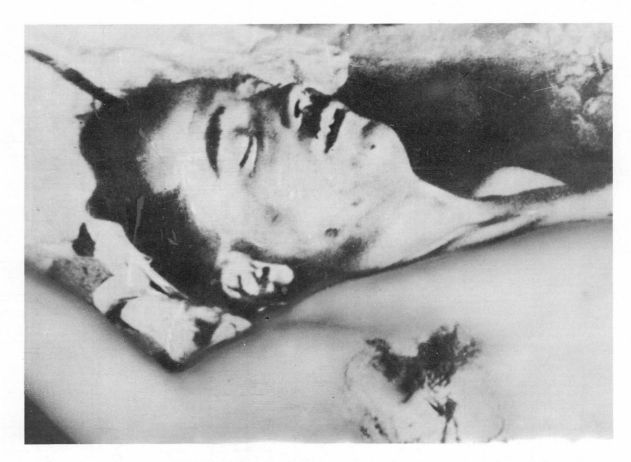

Murdered in his office, Austria's Chancellor Dollfuss lay dying while Nazis refused him medical aid

After Dollfuss, Schuschnigg became Chancellor
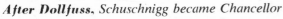

Suddenly, It Was Hitler's Austria

All through the '30s, the Nazis kept beating the drums for an Anschluss, a union between Germany and Austria. In Engelbert Dollfuss, however, Austria had a 4-foot-11 Chancellor who passionately believed in independence. But one sultry July afternoon in 1934, armed Nazis stormed the Chancellery in Vienna and shocked the world by assassinating the courageous little Chancellor. They failed to seize the government and Kurt von Schuschnigg succeeded Dollfuss. Eventually, he announced a plebiscite on March 13, 1938, to determine Austria's future. Hitler wanted no part of this, so he struck quickly. On March 12 the Nazis crossed the border, and one day later German tanks rumbled along Vienna's Ringstrasse. Artur von Seyss-Inquart, an Austrian Nazi, headed the new puppet government and the Rothschild mansion became Gestapo headquarters. Anschluss was achieved. Hitler had made his first armed conquest and Vienna, the glittering Hapsburg jewel, was now only a German provincial town. For Austrians, the Nazi tyranny had come early.

Hundreds of thousands of Austrian and German Nazis roared approval in Vienna as Hitler swept Austria into the Reich

Seyss-Inquart headed up new Nazi regime   **Nazi armor** carried out Hitler's first foreign conquest

HITLER'S EXCUSE

German Populated Areas
Coveted by the Nazis -
1938-1939

© C. S. Hammond & Co.

A Dictator's Appetite—and Appeasement

Now came the sorriest chapter in the long history of British and French appeasement and retreat. Having gobbled up Austria, Hitler picked his next target: Czechoslovakia. This bastion of Wilsonian democracy to the east would be a harder nut to crack. The Czechs had 35 well-equipped divisions, a heavily-fortified frontier, and treaty guarantees from both France and the Soviet Union. But Czechoslovakia also had 3.5 million Sudeten Germans inside her borders. In May 1938, when two Germans were killed in a border dispute, both Czechoslovakia and Germany rushed troops to the frontier. War was close, but when France and the Soviets stood by their ally, Hitler backed down for the moment. France and England were appalled at how close the conflict had come. Four months later, when Hitler demanded that the Sudetenland be ceded to Germany immediately, Czechoslovakia's allies deserted her. At the suggestion of Mussolini, Hitler invited Britain's Chamberlain and French Premier Édouard Daladier to a four-power conference at Munich. The Western leaders gave Der Fuehrer everything he wanted. The Czechs were blandly asked to sign their own death warrant. The Sudetenland was ceded outright to Germany; what remained of Czechoslovakia was defenseless.

In caricatures of the time, Hitler and Chamberlain at Munich

A memorial to the creator of the Maginot Line

Maginot held 300,000 troops underground

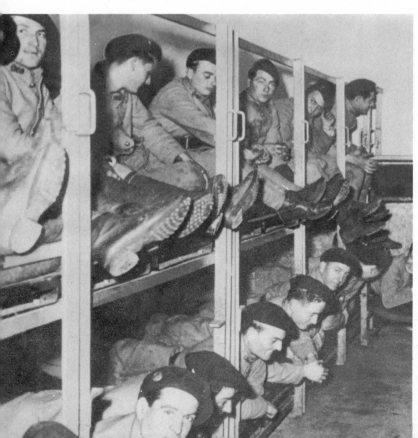

As he left Munich, France's Daladier was despondent. War had been averted, but only in violation of France's firm commitment to Czechoslovakia. Munich meant the destruction of the whole eastern network of alliances France had so painstakingly built. An ally had been sacrificed, but the peace had been preserved. Frenchmen had no will to fight for a foreign nation. If they had to, they would defend their own soil; and at home, so Frenchmen thought, France was impregnable. The most elaborate fortified line of defense ever devised by man— the Maginot Line—stood in Hitler's way. France had no English Channel to protect herself from invasion, but, in 1929, War Minister André Maginot began to construct the best possible substitute—a series of gigantic pillboxes stretching from Switzerland to the Belgian border, costing half a billion dollars.

The Maginot Line was impressive—each pill-

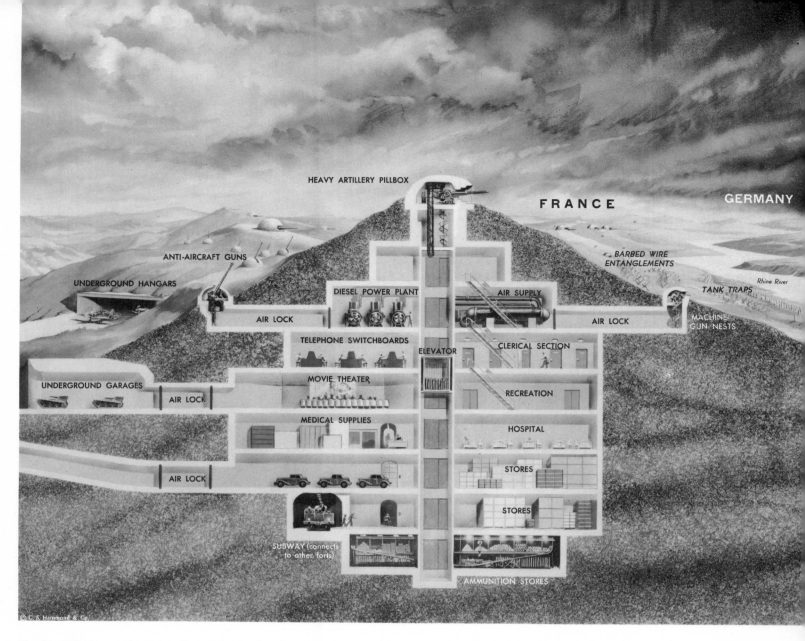

HEAVY ARTILLERY PILLBOX

FRANCE   GERMANY

ANTI-AIRCRAFT GUNS

BARBED WIRE ENTANGLEMENTS

Rhine River

UNDERGROUND HANGARS

TANK TRAPS

DIESEL POWER PLANT   AIR SUPPLY

AIR LOCK   AIR LOCK   MACHINE GUN NESTS

TELEPHONE SWITCHBOARDS   CLERICAL SECTION

UNDERGROUND GARAGES   ELEVATOR

AIR LOCK   MOVIE THEATER   RECREATION

MEDICAL SUPPLIES   HOSPITAL

AIR LOCK   STORES

STORES

SUBWAY (connects to other forts)   AMMUNITION STORES

© C. S. Hammond & Co.

Each pillbox was ingeniously constructed as a self-contained unit, but the Maginot Line had a fatal flaw

box had six underground levels and contained every possible necessity for defense, from power stations and ammunition dumps to hospitals and recreation halls—but a glance at any map of Europe showed its fatal weakness. The historic German invasion route through Belgium and the Ardennes Forest was almost unprotected. Unless Hitler and his generals obligingly mounted a direct frontal attack, the Maginot Line with its giant guns pointed eastward toward the Rhine was virtually useless. The Maginot Line could be flanked with ease. One French officer, a tank commander named Charles de Gaulle, saw this clearly. He pleaded for more tanks, more planes to match the German fast-moving mechanized power. But French strategists put all their faith in the Maginot Line. Paying no heed to the lessons of modern warfare, France confidently prepared to fight World War I all over again.

THE MAGINOT LINE

BELGIUM

Scale of Miles
0 10 20 30 40 50

ARDENNES FOREST

LUXEMBOURG

Trier

"LITTLE MAGINOT LINE" Weakly Fortified

Sedan

MAGINOT

Saarbrücken

G
E
R
M
A
N
Y

Verdun   Metz

F
R
A
N
C
E

LINE

Nancy

Strasbourg   Rhine River

MAGINOT LINE

Rhine

Colmar   Freiburg

Mulhouse

© C. S. Hammond & Co.

SWITZERLAND

179

Returning from Munich, _Chamberlain waves his 'No War' agreement_

Peace-minded England greeted peace-minded Neville Chamberlain on his return from Munich with a national sigh of relief that, or so they believed, the threat of war had somehow vanished. They roared approval of the Munich Pact and cheered when Chamberlain read the guarantee he had gotten Hitler to sign: " 'We regard the Agreement signed last night . . . as symbolic of the desire of our two peoples never to go to war with one another again.' " That night crowds formed outside 10 Downing Street and heard the Prime Minister say he had brought "Peace with honor. I believe it is peace for our time." Relieved Londoners had, just a week before, been digging trenches in preparation for war. There was rejoicing in Berlin, too. Not only had Hitler gotten all that he wanted from the Western powers, but from now on he would have—and show—contempt for the French and British leaders. He had few worries now about the consequences of his war-like actions. He told Daladier and Chamberlain that he had "no further territorial claims to make in Europe," and solemnly agreed to guarantee the new Czech frontier. Just how much his word was worth would soon be made brutally clear to the world.

The House of Commons approved the Chamberlain action by an overwhelming vote, but some, including Winston Churchill, understood the enormity of the West's mistake at Munich. Again, Churchill tried to awaken his countrymen to the fearful dangers abroad: "This is only the first sip, the first foretaste of a bitter cup which will be proffered to us year by year unless, by a supreme recovery of moral health and martial vigor, we arise again and take our stand for freedom."

Standing nearly alone among his countrymen, Winston Churchill saw Munich for what it was—surrender

The end came for Czechoslovakia as silent crowds watched the entry of German troops into Prague

Nazis Himmler and Heydrich, the Czech 'protectors'

The next taste from the bitter cup was not long in coming. Hitler mounted attacks against Czech "atrocities." In his master plot, Slovakia declared its independence from Prague. At this, the aging Czech president, Dr. Emil Hácha, asked to be received by Der Fuehrer. At the meeting, Hitler announced to Hácha's amazement that he had already given orders for the invasion of what was left of Czechoslovakia. Only one thing could prevent bloodshed, said Der Fuehrer. Hácha must ask him to take over the country. Hácha had no choice; he agreed. German tanks rolled into Prague; Czechoslovakia's ordeal began. The brutal Himmler and his sadistic deputy, Reinhard Heydrich, "The Hangman," were given the task of making Czech slave labor turn out the tools of war for the Reich. Finally, the reality smote London and Paris: A madman was loose in Europe. The long-dawdling war effort started in earnest.

The deal between Hitler and Stalin becomes a cynical fact as Foreign Minister Molotov signs
the notorious 'non-aggression' pact, while Ribbentrop (center) and a smiling Stalin look on

Communist *Stalin and Fascist Ribbentrop shake hands*

With Czechoslovakia under his belt, Hitler's next victim seemed made-to-order—Poland. But Poland had received British and French guarantees to march if her independence was violated. On the chance that the two democracies would fight this time, Hitler sought to guard his Eastern flank by negotiations with his arch-enemy, Stalin. For his part, Stalin was suspicious of Hitler's motives but he, too, was playing for time and a chance to grab some more of the world for Russia. And Stalin was not yet ready to go to war; so it was that these two deadly foes, each for his own greedy ends, had reason to strike a bargain, the most cynical in modern diplomacy. On Aug. 23, 1939, to the amazement of an incredulous world, Joachim von Ribbentrop, the Nazi Foreign Minister, signed a ten-year Soviet-German non-aggression pact with Stalin. A secret clause in the dictators' pact cut up Eastern Europe between them. This cold-blooded piece of chicanery gave Hitler a green light to devour Poland—but it also gave the Red Army the opening to move closer to Germany's frontier.

German troops surrounded Warsaw, but the Polish capital resisted in ruins and flames

After the bombardment of the Polish city, ammunition ran out and the city fell

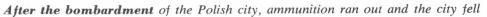

184

In a brief lull during the ferocious bombings of Warsaw, a child rescued a pet canary from the rubble

PARTITION OF POLAND 1939

To Germany
Area-72,400 sq. mi. Population-22,500,000

To U.S.S.R.
Area-77,700 sq. mi. Population-12,700,000

© C. S. Hammond & Co.

The 'Blitz' Unleashed

At dawn on Sept. 1, 1939, the mighty German Army jumped off into Poland without warning. Across the sunbaked Poland plains rolled the motorized columns; overhead flew the terror-bomber, the Stuka, and the world had its first chilling glimpse of the tactics of blitzkrieg—lightning war. The Luftwaffe destroyed Polish aircraft on the ground, disrupted supply lines, pounded defenseless cities. The armored divisions fanned out in broad, encircling pincer movements, leaving the pockets of resistance to be wiped out by artillery and infantry.

On September 17, Russian troops poured into Poland from the east. Poland was mercilessly crushed between the two juggernauts; within a month, it was over. Two days after the invasion, England and France declared war on Germany; but the Western front remained quiet, the combatants settled down to the phony war, the "sitzkrieg."

A huge America First rally in New York's Madison Square Garden protests interventionist measures in 'Europe's war'

Hero Colonel Lindbergh was a speaker

As war flamed over Europe and Asia, Roosevelt was elected to an unprecedented third term. He regarded his victory over Wendell Willkie as a mandate to press on with his policy of preparedness. In this, he was bitterly opposed by the isolationist forces—a powerful group, many of whom were banded together as the America First Committee. In spite of such noted isolationists as Charles A. Lindbergh and Sens. Burton Wheeler and Robert La Follette Jr., Roosevelt mobilized the National Guard; and, in 1940, Congress passed the nation's first peacetime draft law. America was altering her stance of neutralism and was girding her enormous resources to come to the aid of the free world.

KEEP U.S.
OUT OF WAR
BE
NEUTRAL

'We Shall Fight . . .'

The "phony war" lasted only seven months; then Hitler struck again. In April 1940, he hit Denmark and Norway; in May, Holland, Belgium, and Luxembourg. Gathering momentum, the Wehrmacht broke into France, bypassing the "impregnable" Maginot Line. The pincers tightened on trapped Allied forces falling back to Dunkirk and Hitler clenched his iron fist to annihilate them. Then came the miracle. From England, a vast armada crossed the channel and in nine hectic days evacuated 345,585 troops. Days later, France fell; and England stood alone. But Churchill, the new Prime Minister, defiantly told the world: "We shall defend our island whatever the cost may be; we shall fight on the beaches, we shall fight on the landing-grounds, we shall fight in the fields and in the streets, we shall fight in the hills; we shall never surrender."

'Withdrawal from Dunkirk,' history's greatest sea rescue

In less than two months, Hitler inflicted on France her most humiliating defeat; and Frenchmen wept for their country

Embarked aboard the heavy cruiser U.S.S. Augusta (left),President Roosevelt secretly sailed to Newfoundland . .

With Europe in Hitler's thrall, England's chances of staving off the Nazi horde seemed slim. Der Fuehrer offered Britain surrender terms; but Churchill had something altogether different in mind: "It is victory, victory at all costs, victory in spite of all terror; victory, however long and hard the road may be; for without victory, there is no survival." The Battle of Britain was thus enjoined. Through the devastating arm of his Luftwaffe, Hitler planned to obliterate English cities. But Hitler had not reckoned with British determination and with the gallantry of the fliers of the Royal Air Force who rose to fight for the skies. To the United States, Churchill cried: "Give us the tools and we will finish the job." After the first Nazi assault over Britain, America had given England 50 over-age destroyers in return for bases in the Western Hemisphere. And early in 1941 Congress approved Lend-Lease, starting a steadily increasing flow of war materials from the "arsenal of democracy" to the beleaguered British Isles. Anglo-American solidarity was further strengthened when President Roosevelt and Prime Minister Churchill met at Placentia Bay, Newfoundland, Aug. 9, 1941, and drew up the Atlantic Charter which stated the ideals of the two democracies, including "the final destruction of the Nazi tyranny." Soon after, Congress authorized the arming of merchant ships. America was embarked on a program of "all aid short of war," and as the nation pressed closer to conflict, the President himself stated the case for intervention with the words: "Those who would give up essential liberty to purchase a little temporary safety deserve neither liberty nor safety."

Britain-bound, ex-American destroyers on the Atlantic

.. where he met Prime Minister Churchill who arrived on the battleship Prince of Wales (to right)

Atlantic Charter *meeting between Roosevelt and Churchill. In rear, Gen. George Marshall and Adms. Ernest J. King and Harold Stark*

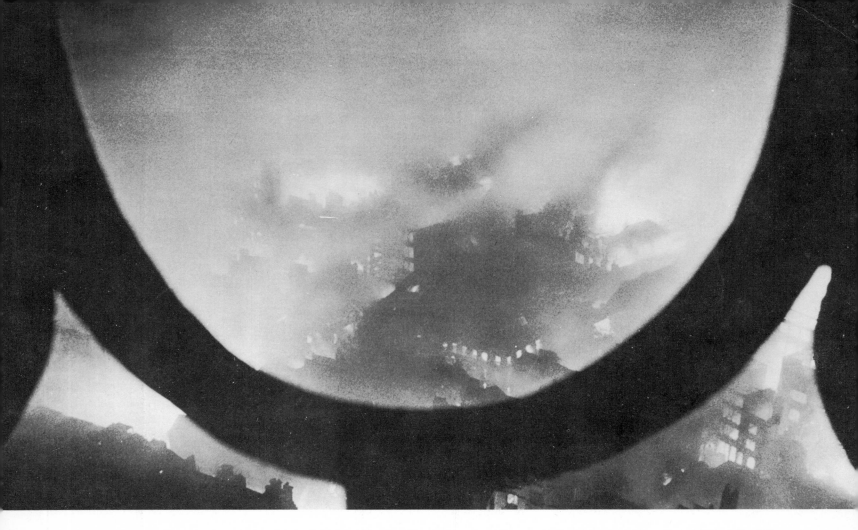

From the sky, *the city of London appeared to be alive with fire after a night air raid in the great Luftwaffe blitz*

In a shattered *Russian village, advancing German troops pause to rest*

190

Out of the Darkness, an Onslaught

For months bombs rained on England, but that brave island withstood the onslaught. Frustrated, Hitler turned south and east. In April 1941, his panzers overran Yugoslavia and Greece. Then, on June 22, against the advice of his high command, Hitler gave the order to invade Russia, and Armageddon, the mightiest clash in the history of war, began. The brilliant German generals utilized mechanized warfare to the fullest. Giant tanks led mobile pincer scythes, trapping Red troops; spearheads of steel raced toward Leningrad, Stalingrad, and Moscow, driving to within sight of the Kremlin's towers. The Russians retreated and, with great skill, used the allies that had served them so well in the past—time, space, and, most of all, winter. The Russian lines bent deeply, but did not break.

During that fall, in the United States, relations with Japan were reaching a crisis. Angered by the American embargo on strategic materials, Japan sent her diplomats to Washington—and prepared to attack. Special Envoy Saburo Kurusu presented a list of demands that included the end of the embargo and full recognition of Japan's Greater East Asia Co-Prosperity Sphere. Secretary of State Cordell Hull countered with a set of completely contrary proposals. Even as negotiations were underway, a Japanese naval striking force was steaming eastward toward the Hawaiian Islands. On the evening of Dec. 6, 1941, Adm. Chuichi Nagumo hoisted the same flag which flew from Togo's flagship at Tsushima, and, in the darkness before dawn the next day, he gave the order to launch planes.

Japanese Ambassador Nomura, Secretary of State Hull, and Japanese Envoy Kurusu in Washington

The Japanese strike, *and Pearl Harbor's Battleship Row is left aflame—a fleet of helpless, battered hulks*

"Air raid, Pearl Harbor—This is no drill." On this sleepy Sunday morning, the radio message crackled across Oahu, as Japanese fighters, bombers, and torpedo planes came winging in, catching America's Pacific bastion unaware and unprepared. In the harbor were 94 Navy ships, but the well-drilled Japanese pilots concentrated on Battleship Row; and within 30 minutes, the wrecked battle line of the Pacific Fleet was settling into the mud. The Navy suffered the worst disaster in its history, but there was one consolation: The vital carriers were safely out at sea. During the grim day of Pearl Harbor, Japan's armies also attacked the Philippines—driving General MacArthur's forces to Bataan and Corregidor where they ultimately surrendered—and then the Emperor's troops invaded all of Southeast Asia. But in the Battle of the Coral Sea, valiant carrier pilots blocked the threat to Australia; and, at Midway, stopped Japan's advance across the Pacific. Then in the muddy jungles of Guadalcanal, the Marines launched America's first major counterattack, thus beginning a hard-fought, island-hopping drive across the Pacific on the bloody road to Tokyo. In Washington, the first priority was assigned to defeating Hitler; and in November 1942, Allied troops landed in North Africa; later pounced on Sicily, and assaulted Italy. On the Eastern Front the Russians held at Stalingrad, and began the massive counteroffensive against the faltering Wehrmacht. And from England, American and British bombers pounded Germany night and day, as Allied military might built up—to storm Hitler's Fortress Europa.

*A **Japanese** artist's view of attack on shipping at Cavite Naval base on Manila Bay*

United States Marines assault enemy air strip in desperate battle for Guadalcanal

On D-Day in Europe, *a wave of infantrymen fight their way ashore through heavy enemy fire to establish Normandy beachhead*

Funeral procession *for the wartime President and Commander*

On the damp, overcast morning of June 6, 1944, the greatest armada in history crossed the English Channel to assault the continent of Europe. Under the command of Gen. Dwight D. Eisenhower, American, British, and Canadian troops poured ashore along a 60-mile front in Normandy. In the bitter fighting that followed, the Allies suffered severe casualties, but they were on the continent to stay. Eight weeks after D-Day, Gen. George Patton's American tanks broke out of Normandy and wheeled across France. The British and Canadians drove into the Low Countries. Another Allied army invaded southern France and raced northward. While Allied divisions pressed toward the Rhine, Russian troops swarmed into eastern Germany, destination Berlin. With German resistance crumbling under these massive assaults, the world was shocked by the death of President Roosevelt on April 12, 1945. The Allies mourned the loss of the wartime leader and hardened their resolve to finish off the Fascist tyranny in Europe, and then Japan.

In Italy, Allied armies cracked the German defenses. Mussolini fled, hoping to reach Switzerland; but near Lake Como, he was seized by partisans and executed. His battered corpse was displayed in Milan, hung by the heels. In Germany, Allied soldiers crossed the Rhine as the Russians besieged Berlin. There, in the basement of the Reich Chancellery, Hitler shot himself. And a few days later, on May 7, 1945, the mighty Third Reich—which was to have lasted 1,000 years—collapsed in ruin and surrender.

Russians on guard at Hitler's bomb-proof bunker under his Chancellery

A soldier examines ditch where Hitler's body was burned with gasoline

Dictator's end—Il Duce's corpse on display

Long after the end of the war, the Russians released a 'documentary' film which purported to show the body of Adolf Hitler

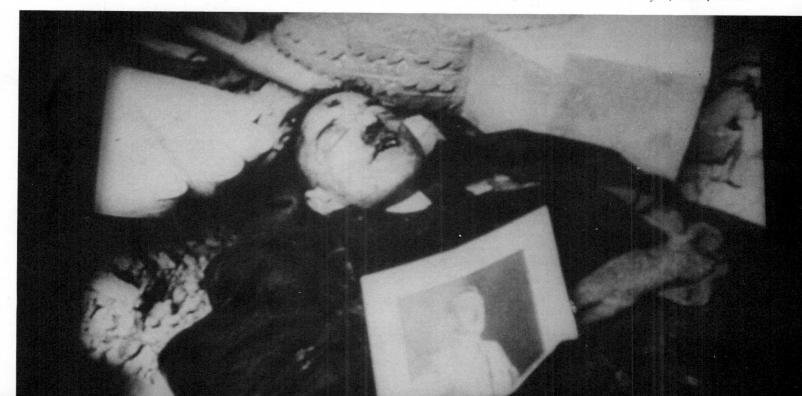

. flanked by Chou En-lai, Chu Teh, Chang Chi-chung, Mao Tse-tung

Chiang Kai-shek *welcomed the general at Nanking*

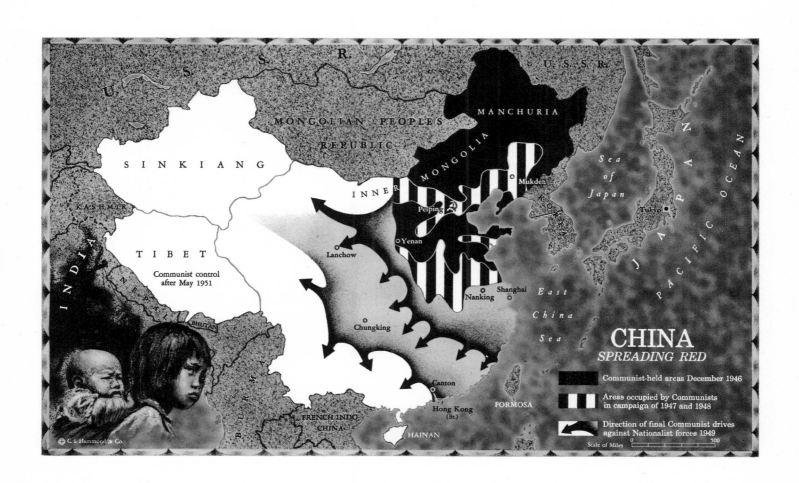

U. S. S. R.

FINLAND
1945- ____

U.

FRANCE
1945-1958

E.
GER.   POL.

CZ.

HUN.

YUGO.   RUM.

ALB.   BUL.

IRAQ
1958

IRAN
1945-1946

ITALY
1945-

MOROCCO
1960- ____

GREECE
1944-1949

U. A. R.
1957- ____

AFGHAN
1954-

CUBA
1959- ____

GUATEMALA
1952-1954

BRIT. GUIANA
1953

GUINEA
1959- ____

YEMEN
1956-

GHANA
1959- ____

CONGO
1960- ____

COMMUNIST EXPANSIONISM

Communist nations

Nations exposed to strong
Communist pressures

Areas of intense
Communist political activity

Areas of armed conflict
involving Communists

© C.S. Hammond & Co.

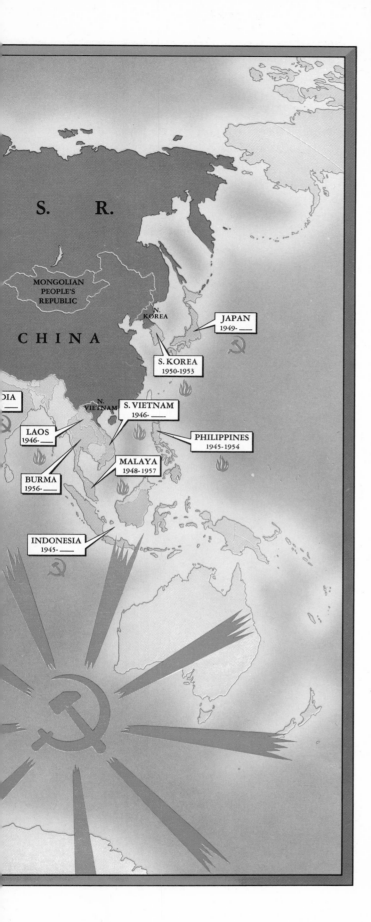

This Was Cold War

Only after years of the hardest kind of fighting had China and her millions fallen to the Communists. But in Europe, country after country moved into the Red orbit virtually without the firing of a shot. Moscow subversion and propaganda spread the Cold War—"cold" because men's wills, rather than their bodies, were broken in the march of Red conquest. Cold War was also a war of nerves, eminently suited to the stealthy, conscienceless talents of the Soviet dictator, Joseph Stalin—a war little understood by the Western democracies, but one they would have to wage if they were not to lose the whole world to Communism.

The wartime alliance against the common Fascist enemy had obscured the changeless aims of Soviet Communism, but even before the Nazi surrender, Stalin was laying plans to fix a brand of Marxism on free nations—great and small. By the time the West realized that Russia had no intention of acting in good faith to secure the peace, all of Eastern Europe was under Communist control. At the Yalta Conference, Stalin had agreed to free elections in the liberated nations, but when they were held, hundreds of thousands of Russian troops policed the casting of the ballots. So, by such a vote and swiftly executed Red coups d'état, Poland, Hungary, Czechoslovakia, Rumania, Albania, Bulgaria, and Yugoslavia fell under Communism. In Western Europe, where the Kremlin did not have the force of occupying troops, it sent Moscow-trained agents and politicians to subvert the democratic governments. In Italy and France, the Communists were never strong enough to win control, but for years they created political chaos, the murky climate in which their sycophants had always flourished.

The world divided into two unalterably opposed armed camps. At times, when it suited Soviet strategy, it seemed the Cold War might thaw. Again and again, hopes for a lasting peace were raised only to be smashed by Communist intractability. As the Reds probed for weak spots to exploit—from Berlin to Laos, from Egypt to Cuba—the West had to gird itself; to build a great deterrent force to prevent Red conquest everywhere. Slowly, it became clear that any attempt at compromise with the masters of the Kremlin was an invitation to disaster.

The same clear voice which had so eloquently and accurately warned of the threat of Hitler's Germany in the '30s, was the first to sound the alarm against the postwar Communist threat. In the British general election of 1945, Winston Churchill had lost the Prime Ministership to Laborite Clement Attlee, but this bitter disappointment did not obscure Churchillian vision. Less than a year later, in his famous "Iron Curtain" speech at Fulton, Mo., Churchill called upon the Western democracies to join their strength in the face of the rising Communist menace; he told the free world that the Russians respected might, "and there is nothing for which they have less respect than for weakness, especially military weakness." The speech shocked many who feared offending the Russians, but the world did not have to wait long for events to prove the great British leader right again.

Red Russia was, in fact, already aware of democratic "weaknesses." By 1946 Greece was in danger of falling behind the Iron Curtain. Over 25,000 Red guerrillas roamed the country at will, and it seemed the democratic regime in Athens could not long survive. But the democracies reacted quickly. American President Harry S. Truman announced a plan

Maj. Gen. James A. Van Fleet *helped defeat the Greek rebels*

Greek government *forces mount attack on a Red stronghold*

to give $400 million in aid to Greece and Turkey. Under the Truman Doctrine, American-made tanks and equipment soon flowed in a steady stream to the beleaguered anti-Red forces in Greece. And to lead the battle against the Communist guerrillas, President Truman dispatched a military commission headed by Maj. Gen. James A. Van Fleet, battle-hardened campaigner who had distinguished himself in the Normandy landings. Within two years the civil strife was at an end; the few remaining Reds retreated across the border into Bulgaria and Albania. Greece was saved from Communism.

But the desperate postwar needs of the larger prostrate European nations posed a mighty problem. Once again, the United States acted quickly and effectively. President Truman's Secretary of State, Gen. George C. Marshall, proposed a plan of massive rehabilitation. Under the Marshall Plan, or European Recovery Program, billions of dollars were made available to help Europe help itself. The money was a wise investment. Western Europe not only recovered, but the political "invasion" by Communism into free powers—particularly France and Italy—had been stopped in its tracks.

George C. Marshall at Harvard, inaugurating 'aid to Europe' plan

Winston Churchill as he delivered his 'Iron Curtain' speech at Fulton, Mo.

Russia and her satellites, as well as Western Europe, were invited to join the Marshall Plan, but the Communists refused, branding it imperialism. Then began an intensive, Moscow-directed propaganda campaign to discredit the American efforts. But sixteen nations with a population of 270 million hastened to accept badly needed help. The war had depleted livestock herds, and severe droughts had further cut food production. Before it could concentrate on industrial recovery, Europe had to be fed. Shipments of food, livestock, and agricultural equipment began to flow across the Atlantic. By the end of 1948, the very real threat of a starving Europe was over.

American jeeps are loaded for delivery overseas

In Paris, the East and the West fought the 'Battle of the Billboards'

Cows sent from the United States provided milk for hungry Italians

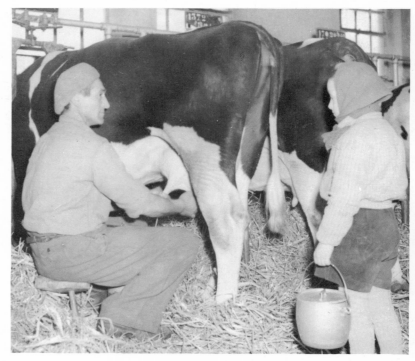

. *as the Communists waged a fight to discredit all forms of American aid*

American dollars *helped to build this French hydroelectric plant*

Sacks *of Marshall Plan food are unloaded in Belgium*

"Dollars alone will not save the world, but it cannot be saved without dollars." So said General Marshall of the European Recovery Program. Within a decade, the Marshall Plan and successor programs had provided $50 billion in aid, the bulk of it to Europe. Their morale bolstered, their fields restored, and their industry beginning to hum again, the Western European nations recovered rapidly. Not all problems were solved—the United States had hoped for greater European unity and political stability—but the chief objective was achieved: The westward march of Communism was halted and Western Europe could be counted a more effective force in preventing Red war.

In Milan, Italy, *a huge Communist rally*

The hope of victory at the polls fading, the strident voices of the rabble-rousing Communist leaders—Maurice Thorez and Jacques Duclos in France, Palmiro Togliatti in Italy—rose to a din as they tried to stem the steady stream of workers deserting the party. They fought a losing battle. With this setback, the Soviet stepped up the pressure in another area. The four allied powers—the United States, Britain, France, Russia—had agreed that, pending a final peace treaty, both Germany and Austria would be divided into four allied zones of occupation. In time, an Austrian treaty was written and the occupying forces withdrew. But Germany was another matter. Headquarters for the occupation forces was Berlin, and although the German capital lay deep in the Russian zone, each of the four powers governed a part of the city (see map, page 221). When conferences on German unification failed to produce agreement, the Western powers decided to ignore the Russians and effect an economic union of their zones.

In reprisal, the Russians clamped a blockade on Berlin, closing the highways and railroads the West used to supply the city. With this action, the 2,250,000 Berliners living in the allied sectors, many of them refugees from the harsh rule in the Soviet zone, faced starvation. But under the leadership of the American Military Governor, Gen. Lucius D. Clay, the West refused to be intimidated. The most gigantic airlift in history began. At the peak of "Operation Vittles," a plane a minute landed at Berlin's Tempelhof Airfield carrying precious cargoes of food and fuel. For their part, stubborn Berliners under the leadership of their courageous mayor, Ernst Reuter, refused to buckle under the Communist pressure. After eleven months of blockade had failed to dislodge the Western forces, the Russians admitted defeat and lifted the restrictions. Nothing was settled—the question of divided Germany would remain a focal point in the Cold War for years to come—but defiant Berlin remained a tiny oasis of freedom behind the Iron Curtain.

Jacques Duclos, *the French Communist leader, harangues an audience in a Paris suburb during national elections*

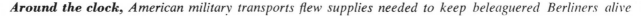

Soldiers of the Big Four patrol occupied Vienna

At East German checkpoints during the blockade, Communists halted the flow of American supply convoys into isolated Berlin

Around the clock, American military transports flew supplies needed to keep beleaguered Berliners alive

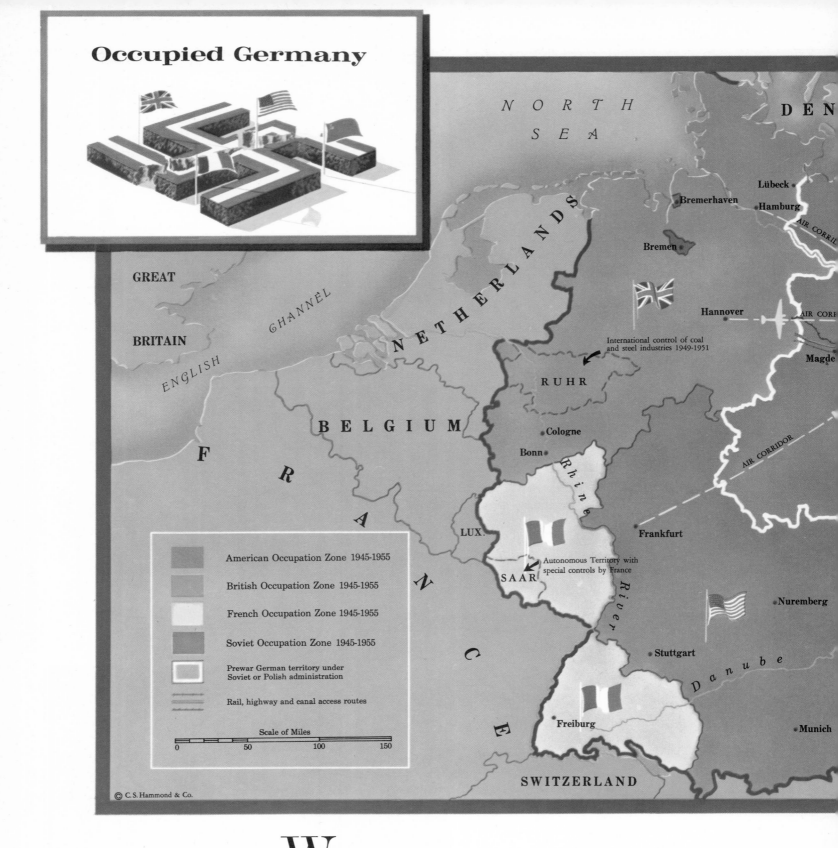

Occupied Germany

NORTH SEA

DEN

GREAT BRITAIN

ENGLISH CHANNEL

NETHERLANDS

BELGIUM

FRANCE

LUX.

SWITZERLAND

Lübeck
Bremerhaven
Hamburg
Bremen
Hannover
Magde
International control of coal and steel industries 1949-1951
RUHR
AIR CORRI
AIR CORR
AIR CORRIDOR
Cologne
Bonn
Rhine
Frankfurt
SAAR
Autonomous Territory with special controls by France
Nuremberg
Stuttgart
Danube River
Freiburg
Munich

American Occupation Zone 1945-1955

British Occupation Zone 1945-1955

French Occupation Zone 1945-1955

Soviet Occupation Zone 1945-1955

Prewar German territory under Soviet or Polish administration

Rail, highway and canal access routes

Scale of Miles
0   50   100   150

© C.S. Hammond & Co.

When Russia, occupying East Germany, refused to countenance a unified Germany except on her own terms, the Western powers decided to create a separate German state, and on Aug. 14, 1949, West Germany held her first free election since the fateful day in 1933 when Adolf Hitler vaulted into the Chancellorship. The head of the conservative Christian Democratic Union party, Konrad Adenauer, twice jailed by the Nazis and already an elder statesman (he was 73 then), was elected Chancellor of the new West German Federal Republic. The Russians countered by setting up a puppet government in East Germany. Now the prospect of a unified Germany was further off than ever. But there was little doubt which of the two regimes the Germans themselves preferred: The number of refugees fleeing East Germany reached 500,000 a year.

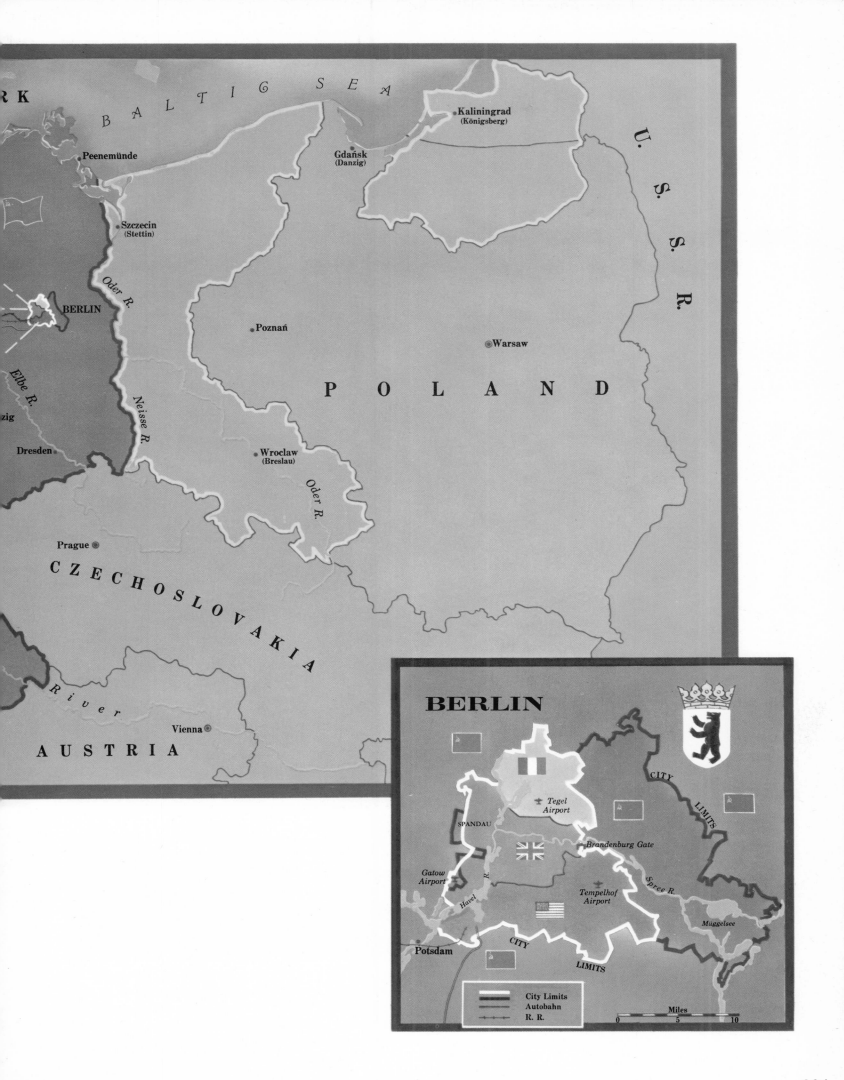

B A L T I C   S E A

RK

Peenemünde

Szczecin
(Stettin)

Oder R.

BERLIN

Elbe R.

zig

Neisse R.

Dresden

Kaliningrad
(Königsberg)

Gdańsk
(Danzig)

U. S. S. R.

Poznań

Warsaw

P O L A N D

Wroclaw
(Breslau)

Oder R.

Prague

C Z E C H O S L O V A K I A

River

Vienna

A U S T R I A

BERLIN

Tegel
Airport

SPANDAU

Gatow
Airport

Havel R.

Brandenburg Gate

Spree R.

Tempelhof
Airport

CITY

LIMITS

Müggelsee

Potsdam

CITY

LIMITS

	City Limits
	Autobahn
	R. R.

Miles

0   5   10

Before his break *with Moscow, Yugoslav dictator Marshal Tito works with Stalin's portrait above him*

At NATO, a French officer, Field Marshal Montgomery, General Eisenhower, Admiral Carney

West German Chancellor Konrad Adenauer

A Crack—and an Alliance

While Russia was meeting with setbacks in Germany, she received an even more severe blow from an unexpected quarter. Yugoslavia's Marshal Tito, the resourceful guerrilla fighter who had wrested his country from Nazi control, refused to subordinate himself to the Cominform (the Communist policy-setting organization) which then accused him of "nationalistic deviation" and expelled him. The West moved to exploit the break by bolstering the Yugoslav economy. But the hope that others would follow Tito's example was in vain. In the other satellites, the familiar purge trials began. Moscow, for the moment, prevented further defections.

Not all the Soviet's troubles were home-brewed. On April 4, 1949, emissaries from nine European nations, the United States, Canada, and Iceland met in Washington to sign a military alliance. The Atlantic Pact, or North Atlantic Treaty Organization, served notice on Russia that further aggression in Europe would be met with all the force the free world could bring to bear in its defense.

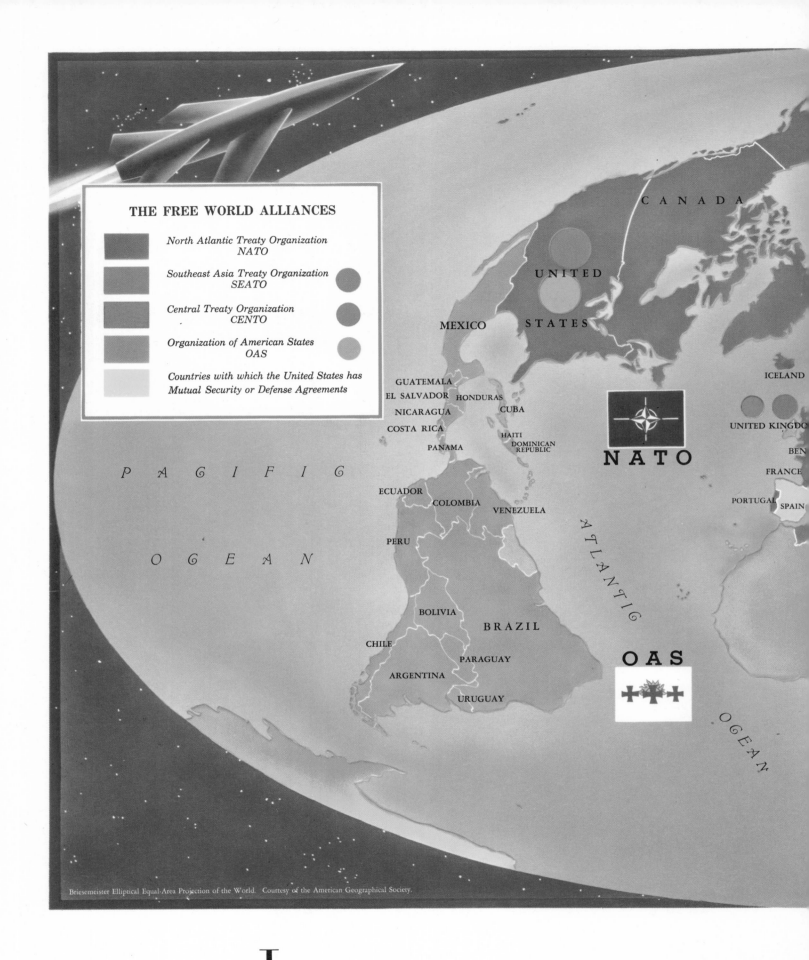

THE FREE WORLD ALLIANCES

North Atlantic Treaty Organization
NATO

Southeast Asia Treaty Organization
SEATO

Central Treaty Organization
CENTO

Organization of American States
OAS

Countries with which the United States has
Mutual Security or Defense Agreements

CANADA

UNITED STATES

MEXICO

GUATEMALA
EL SALVADOR   HONDURAS
NICARAGUA   CUBA
COSTA RICA
HAITI
PANAMA   DOMINICAN
REPUBLIC

ECUADOR
COLOMBIA
VENEZUELA

PERU

BOLIVIA   BRAZIL
CHILE
PARAGUAY
ARGENTINA
URUGUAY

PACIFIC

OCEAN

ATLANTIC

OCEAN

ICELAND

UNITED KINGDO

BEN

FRANCE

PORTUGAL   SPAIN

NATO

OAS

Briesemeister Elliptical Equal-Area Projection of the World. Courtesy of the American Geographical Society.

I t was imperative that free world alliances of defense be set up everywhere.
The North Atlantic Treaty Organization (NATO), was only the first in
the series the West mobilized to contain threatening Communist power. To
come were the Southeast Asia Treaty Organization (SEATO), to prevent
Communist aggression in Asia; and the Central Treaty Organization
(CENTO), to protect the strategic Middle East from Red incursion. In the

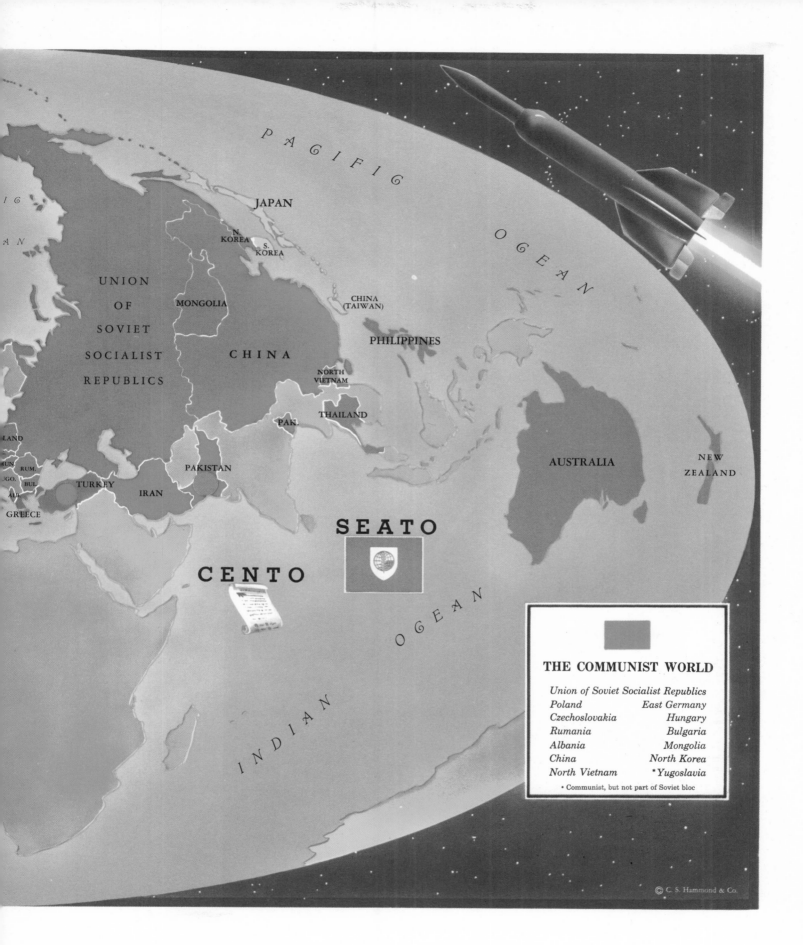

PACIFIC OCEAN

JAPAN

N. KOREA

S. KOREA

UNION

OF

SOVIET

SOCIALIST

REPUBLICS

MONGOLIA

CHINA

CHINA
(TAIWAN)

PHILIPPINES

NORTH
VIETNAM

THAILAND

PAK.

PAKISTAN

AUSTRALIA

NEW
ZEALAND

TURKEY

IRAN

GREECE

LAND

HUN.

RUM.

UGO.

BUL

ALB.

SEATO

CENTO

INDIAN OCEAN

© C. S. Hammond & Co.

THE COMMUNIST WORLD

Union of Soviet Socialist Republics
Poland   *East Germany*
Czechoslovakia   *Hungary*
Rumania   *Bulgaria*
Albania   *Mongolia*
China   *North Korea*
North Vietnam   **Yugoslavia*

* Communist, but not part of Soviet bloc

Western Hemisphere, the United States took the lead in forming still another kind of counterforce. This was the Organization of American States (OAS), designed to promote inter-American cooperation. On the Communist side, Russia drew her European satellites into the Warsaw Pact. Its purpose was simple: To oppose the West. At the same time Russia continued to build her military might, and strengthened her ties with China. Two superpowers dominated most of the globe, but gradually a third force—the neutral nations—began to make itself felt.

Like his prophet *Gandhi, Jawaharlal Nehru assumed the leadership of India's millions*

226

'Holy One'—and Neutralism

In the intricate web of alliances that characterized the Cold War, there was one notable abstainer—India. In 1947, that vast subcontinent of 400 million people had been one of the first countries to undergo the postwar surge of nationalism. Britain had granted independence to India and His Majesty's troops and viceroy set sail for England. For years, Indians had resented the humiliations and social inferiority of imperialism; and, in the 1930s, there developed a popular movement for self-government led by the venerated Mohandas K. Gandhi, the Mahatma, or Holy One. Educated in England, Gandhi devoted his life to the cause of Indian self-government, economic independence, and greater tolerance among the many castes and sects. The weapons Gandhi chose were spiritual: Non-violence, passive resistance, civil disobedience, hunger strikes, and boycott. But uniting the diverse and violent groups in India proved an impossible undertaking and in the end there was no unification. The country was split between Hindu India and Moslem Pakistan. And in the year following Indian independence, Gandhi was assassinated by an anti-Moslem Hindu fanatic.

With Gandhi's death, Prime Minister Jawaharlal Nehru became the leader of India's millions. Nehru set for himself a task of Herculean proportions: To lift India by the bootstraps from the grinding poverty that kept millions in virtual starvation. Yet, difficult as that job was, Nehru had further ambitions: To become the leader of the neutrals, the uncommitted nations in the Cold War.

Seeing himself as the voice of Asia and the founding father of neutralism, Nehru hoped to play a major role in international diplomacy. He paid calls to Washington and Moscow and received Premier Chou En-lai in New Delhi. But whatever hopes Nehru had of taming the Red dragon of Peking were rudely shattered by Chinese attacks on India's northern border. And though Nehru enjoyed more personal power and prestige than any ruler in India's history, his reluctance to name or train a successor increased the chances that upon his death India would be rent by the dozens of ethnic groups that make up this dizzyingly diverse and mystic nation.

In Moscow, *Nehru and Premier Bulganin review honor guard*

In New Delhi, *Nehru receives Red China's Premier Chou En-lai*

In Washington, *Nehru visits President and Mrs. Eisenhower*

Rising above squalor, New Delhi's modern Ashoka Hotel dominates the skyline

Hindus at prayer reflect a powerful and, at times, divisive force in Indian life

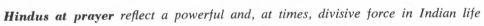

India's Damodar Valley hydroelectric project—power for growing industry

As the British had foreseen, Indian independence was accompanied by widespread bloodshed. The partitioning of India—with Pakistan lying in two sections 1,000 miles apart—resulted in mass expulsions and the deaths of thousands. Even after a semblance of peace had been restored between India and Pakistan, the Kashmir border dispute was a constant irritation to both nations. And always beneath the surface, the tensions among the myriad linguistic and religious groups remained an unhappy fact of life in the huge subcontinent. Tackling India's almost insolvable economic problems, Nehru launched three Five Year Plans, hoping to keep food production moving ahead of the exploding population and to bring the industrial economy to the point where it could become self-generating. What Nehru sought to prove to Asia was that economic progress could be made without sacrificing democracy. At stake was the survival of independence in the turbulent, teeming land of Mahatma Gandhi.

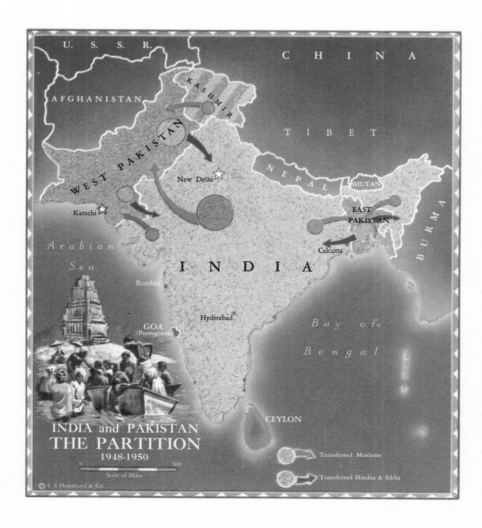

INDIA and PAKISTAN
THE PARTITION
1948-1950

Transferred Moslems

Transferred Hindus & Sikhs

With the backing of the United Nations, Indonesian President Achmed Sukarno won fight for independence from the Dutch

Forced to leave, a refugee weeps

A tragic by-product of independence; Dutch families flee their island homes

In all of Southeast Asia, colonial empires were vanishing. The United States granted the Philippines full independence in 1946. The new nation was blessed with a superb leader in President Ramon Magsaysay (photo, above); but tragically, he was killed in a plane crash, his work uncompleted. Inspired by his leadership, however, the former Spanish colony became an outpost of democracy in the Orient.

In 1949, the reign of the Netherlands East Indies came to an end when the Dutch, after bitter dissension and actual hostilities, finally yielded independence to Indonesia.

Elsewhere, Britain's former colonies, Burma, Ceylon, and Malaya gained freedom; and the complex of French Indochina was divided into Vietnam, Laos, and Cambodia—an area destined to become sorely troublesome in the years ahead. Thus, in the Far East, European imperial grandeur dwindled to the British Crown Colony of Hong Kong and a few scattered areas under European control.

To the north, the former Japanese vassal state of Chosen was split at the 38th Parallel into North and South Korea. Established under the aegis of the United Nations, South Korea was coveted by the Soviet-sponsored North Korean regime, and conflict was in the making.

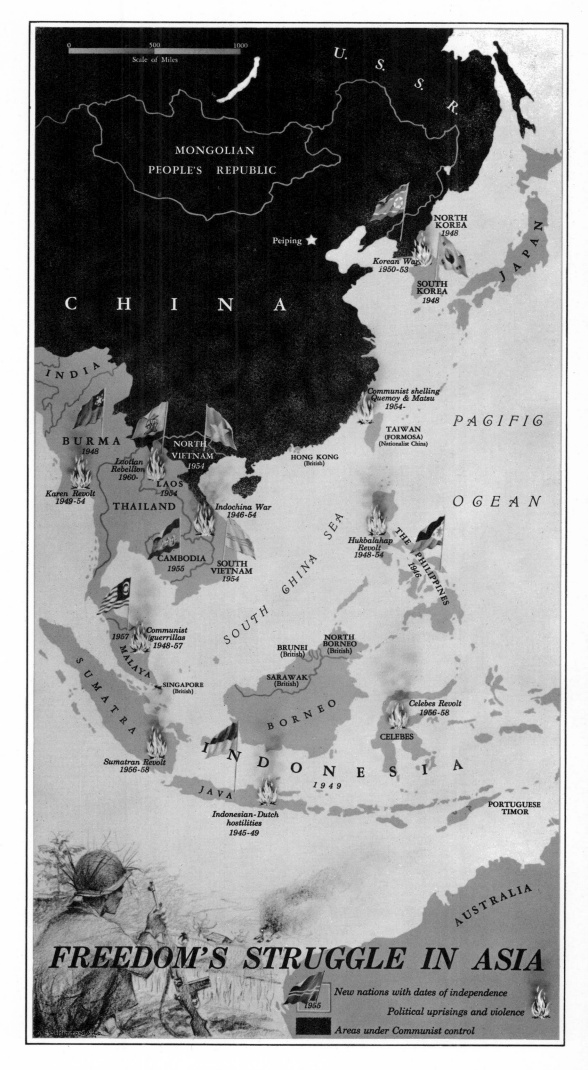

FREEDOM'S STRUGGLE IN ASIA

New nations with dates of independence

Political uprisings and violence

Areas under Communist control

Off Inchon, *Gen. Douglas MacArthur with Adm. Arthur Struble*

Cruiser *U.S.S. Rochester opens fire .*

Red Arms Burst in the East

On a Sunday morning—June 25, 1950—the Cold War suddenly erupted into a hot war as 100,000 North Korean troops swarmed across the 38th Parallel into South Korea. Promptly President Truman called upon the United Nations to take military measures against the aggressors, and committed American combat units to South Korea. But U.N. forces, under the command of Gen. Douglas MacArthur, were hurled back to a precarious perimeter around Pusan. Then, while American military might built up, MacArthur launched a daring amphibious attack on Inchon far behind the North Korean lines, and quickly retook all of South Korea. MacArthur ordered the U.N. Army into North Korea and his divisions raced for the Yalu River on the Manchurian border. Chinese armies, already poised for attack, entered the war. The Chinese move sent U.N. forces into a second retreat: The United States 1st Marine Division, surrounded at Chosin Reservoir, fought to the sea in a historic march. Regrouping in South Korea, the U.N. troops under Gen. Matthew Ridgeway again turned the tide.

The entry of the Chinese created a sharp controversy over bombing Communist bases in China herself. Fearing such a move would spread the war, most U.N. members and Washington opposed it. Heatedly, MacArthur disagreed, and in April 1951, President Truman relieved him of command.

. as a heavy naval bombardment helps prepare the way for the brilliant amphibious landing at Inchon which turned the tide of battle

Surrounded by Chinese soldiers, buffeted by sub-zero weather, the U.S. 1st Marine Division fought its way to the sea

233

Fulfilling a campaign promise, President-elect Dwight D. Eisenhower flew to Korea and visited troops at the front

Red truce negotiator, General Nam Il

By the summer of 1951, the Korean War had developed into a stalemate on a front approximating the original boundary. In July, truce talks began. The negotiations dragged on for two years; the major disagreement was over the repatriation of prisoners. Thousands of captured Red troops had asked for asylum; and the United States would not repatriate any prisoner against his wishes.

In the United States, the stalemate was becoming increasingly unpopular; and during the Presidential campaign of 1952, Eisenhower promised "I will go to Korea" if elected. After his inauguration, he stepped up negotiations. The Reds, who had taken a drubbing from General Ridgeway's fine Eighth Army, wanted no more of it. Finally, in July 1953, a truce was signed. Prisoners who refused repatriation would be placed in the custody of a neutral commission. During the dramatic exchange of prisoners, Americans were troubled to learn that hundreds of American soldiers—after Communist brainwashing—had collaborated in various degrees with their captors, 21 Americans choosing to remain behind in China.

Frustrating as was the Korean War to most Americans, nevertheless it served to show the Communists that the free world had the mettle to resist with force an aggressor nation. The West *would* draw the line.

THE FIRST NINETY DAYS

CHINA

NORTH KOREA

P'yŏngyang ▲ ● Wonsan

SEA OF JAPAN

USSR.

38° — — — — — 38°

Seoul ▲

SOUTH KOREA

YELLOW

Taegu

SEA

Pusan

JAPAN

1 North Korean military buildup heavily supported by Russia and Red China.

2 Invasion of South Korea June 25, 1950 — U. N. intervened June 27, 1950.

3 U. S. units from Japan overrun in delaying actions of July 1950.

4 U. N. forces hold Pusan defense perimeter Aug.-Sept. 1950.

Scale of Miles
0 50 100 150 200

© C. S. Hammond & Co.

THREE YEARS OF WAR

CHINA

NORTH KOREA

P'yŏngyang ▲ ● Wonsan

SEA OF JAPAN

USSR.

Yalu R.

Inchon

Seoul ▲

SOUTH KOREA

YELLOW

Taegu

SEA

Pusan

JAPAN

3 Chinese Communists intervened Nov. 25, 1950 and defeated U. N. forces in North Korea.

2 U. N. forces advanced into North Korea and reached the Yalu R. Oct. 1950.

5 Truce line July 27, 1953, following second U. N. drive and period of Armistice talks Nov. 1951 — July 1953.

4 Chinese Communist invasion of South Korea halted Jan. 24, 1951.

1 Inchon landing and U. N. advance liberated South Korea; Seoul taken Sept. 26, 1950.

© C. S. Hammond & Co.

When the truce was finally signed, *a dramatic exchange of prisoners took place at Panmunjom—here, an American regains his freedom*

French Foreign Legion *paratroops fought a losing battle against Ho Chi-minh's forces*

The armistice in Korea barely secured, the bitter fighting in Indochina intensified. For years, the French had tried to suppress the Communist forces in Vietnam led by the formidable rebel Ho Chi-minh. But fed by the Red colossus of China, Communist power slowly spread through northern Indochina. The siege and fall of the French fortress Dienbienphu set off a crisis in Paris—many Frenchmen deeply resented the drain on men and material in the frustrating far-off jungle war. In America, too, opinion was divided over sending troops into Indochina; Britain was opposed to intervention. And many Asian nations saw in the French cause vestiges of colonialism. Finally, in July 1954, talks in Geneva produced an armistice: Indochina was split at the 17th Parallel into Communist North and anti-Communist South Vietnam. Thus, like Germany and Korea, the little Asian nation remained divided, and like Korea, a potential source of war.

Generalissimo Chiang Kai-shek observes the infantry maneuvers of his Nationalist Chinese troops on Formosa

On Formosa, Chiang Kai-shek kept 500,000 troops under arms, a force too weak to reconquer the mainland, yet a persistent irritant to Red China. The United States had guaranteed the security of Formosa, but left the fate of the Nationalist-held off-shore islands in doubt—another situation that could lead to war.

A well-trained Nationalist soldier drills

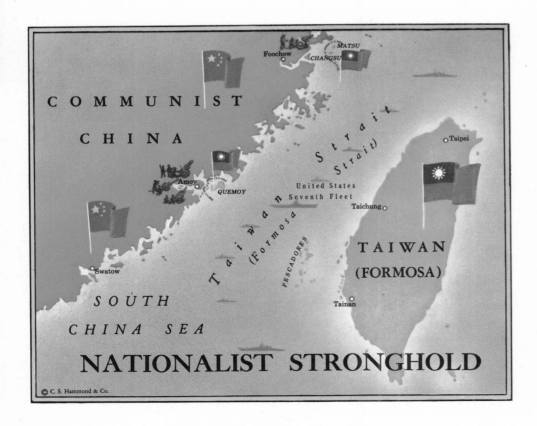

COMMUNIST

CHINA

SOUTH

CHINA SEA

NATIONALIST STRONGHOLD

© C. S. Hammond & Co.

Stalin's Death—the Power Struggle

On March 6, 1953, the 31-year reign of Joseph Stalin ended with his death. The Kremlin was then torn apart by an internal tug of war in which secret police chief Lavrenti Beria was among those executed. Stalin's first successor as Prime Minister and party secretary was Georgi Malenkov, who held on to the important post of party secretary for only nine days. He was replaced in this vital post by an old party hand of sturdy peasant stock named Nikita Sergeevich Khrushchev.

Although Khrushchev shrewdly remained in the background, by 1955 he was powerful enough to oust Malenkov and install Nikolai Bulganin as Premier. Then, in February of 1956, an event of stunning impact took place in the Soviet Union: Khrushchev's six-hour speech to the 1,400 assembled members of the 20th Communist Party Congress. In an amazing torrent of words, Russia's new strongman denounced Stalin in the harshest terms, calling him a "criminal murderer," and a "purveyor of moral and physical an-

Lenin and Stalin *lie in state in Moscow's huge Red Square mausoleum*

nihilation." In his polemic, Khrushchev declared that war between capitalism and Communism was not inevitable, though Communism would ultimately triumph.

The following year—in 1957—Khrushchev further entrenched himself by drumming out of the Communist Central Committee such stalwarts as Malenkov, Foreign Minister Vyacheslav Molotov, First Deputy Premier Lazar Kaganovich, and Defense Minister Georgi Zhukov. And in 1958, Khrushchev himself became Premier.

During the post-Stalin years, Russia relaxed many restrictions in Soviet life and demonstrated a more cooperative spirit toward the West. The era of improved international relations reached a high point at the "summit" meeting in Geneva when the heads of the United States, Great Britain, France and the Soviet Union gathered to discuss world problems. But the Big Four failed to translate their proclamations of a new tranquillity into concrete solutions to problems. And in the aftermath of Geneva came a hardening of the Soviet mood toward the West—a mood which brought disillusionment to a world hungering for peace.

Nikita S. Khrushchev, *the new man of Russia*

Red rulers *atop Lenin's tomb in 1937 (top); the lineup 20 years later (bottom)*

The Worst Weapon—the H-Bomb

The world had trembled when the tremendous mushroom-shaped clouds hovered over the ruins of Hiroshima and Nagasaki in the grim dawn of the atomic age. But this was only a beginning in invention for mass destruction. Man had unlocked the energy of the atom, a power that could be used for unlimited destruction or for peaceful purposes in nuclear fuel and medical research. More was to come. Unhappily, the Cold War forced the United States to concentrate on nuclear weapons of all sizes for varying tactical purposes, stockpiling them as a deterrent to aggression. In 1949, America's atomic monopoly was broken by the Soviet Union (with her theft of American secrets) and the atomic race between the great powers began. Testing of bombs brought global fears since the explosions released large quantities of radioactive particles, or fallout, which could kill or maim.

In 1950, President Truman made a fateful decision regarding atomic might. He ordered scientists to proceed with the development of the hydrogen bomb, a device which by bringing together hydrogen atoms—as the sun itself does—could release quantities of energy dwarfing even an A-bomb. In 1952, over a Pacific atoll in the Marshall Islands, hydrogen fusion occurred in a stupendous fireball (opposite page). A year later, Russia set off her own hydrogen bomb; Britain soon joined the "nuclear club," as did France. With rapid strides in technology, scientists predicted a "cheap bomb" might ultimately be fashioned by any of a score of lesser nations.

Most thoughtful men realized the desperate need for some kind of atomic weapons control; but all attempts at negotiating nuclear limitation or disarmament long foundered on the Soviet Union's rejection of a meaningful inspection system. As the arsenal of atomic weapons continued to grow, the world wondered whether any combatant could survive a nuclear war, whether there could be such a thing as a victor. The apocalyptic vision of a third world war fought with atomic weapons led many military experts to insist on strengthening the weapons of limited or conventional wars, which were more likely to be fought—though there were those who questioned whether such wars could always be contained. And the increased availability of atomic weapons vastly increased the chance that some dreadful miscalculation could accidentally set off a hydrogen holocaust.

These were the problems that beset man in the nuclear age. Through trial and error, he had reached a new world; its key was a weapon staggering in its potentialities. With the unlocked atom he now had the power to wipe his kind from the face of the earth—or ineffably to benefit the human race. A central question of the age, then, was this: Would he use his unique and marvelous brain for death or for life?

British paratroops land in Egypt during the English-French-Israeli attack on Nasser's Suez Canal

Tanks of the 2nd Israeli Armored Division advance across the Negeb desert during attack on Egypt

TROUBLED MIDDLE EAST

Oilfields · · · → Pipelines

Scale of Miles 0 500

© C.S. Hammond & Co.

Nowhere was the danger of war more frightening than in the churning Middle East. Against a background of violent Arab and Jewish nationalism, the West sought desperately to preserve its huge stake in Mideast oil while Russia strove to infiltrate and subvert. In 1948, the Jews had achieved their dream of a Palestine homeland, but only after bitter conflict with Moslem armies. Even after establishment of the Jewish state of Israel, Arab leaders, like Egypt's fiery Gamal Abdel Nasser, threatened to push the Jews into the sea. Nasser, who in the '50s received increasing amounts of Soviet aid, also turned his wrath on the West. In 1956, after he nationalized the British-controlled Suez Canal, Britain and France joined Israel in invading Egypt. The operation, a military success, was a diplomatic fiasco. Under pressure from the U.N. and the United States, which had not been consulted in advance of the attack, the three powers withdrew. The adventure had merely served to strengthen Nasser's hand among millions of Moslems.

Premier David Ben-Gurion *led Israel's long struggle for independence*

Egypt's Gamal Abdel Nasser, *leading spokesman of Arab nationalism*

The Hungarian revolt: A bust of Stalin is toppled in the street

Anti-Red rebels march in Budapest to celebrate their 'independence'

The Russians return, a tank fires point-blank at Freedom Fighters

At the end, exhausted Hungarians flee across the border into Austria

In this vivid sketch 'Hungarian Rhapsody'

The Massacre .

At the moment of the Suez attack, the world was confronted with a bloody example of Russian cynicism and brutality in a presumably independent nation—Hungary. Any shred of believability in a new "soft" Kremlin policy was destroyed. "Softness" abroad gave way to hardness toward the Soviet satellites. In 1953, Russian tanks had quelled stone-throwing rioters in East Germany. In Poland, hundreds of strikers had been killed and wounded in riots at Poznań. Fearful of more outbursts, Russia gave a slight measure of freedom to Poland. In Hungary student-led anti-Communist demonstrations grew until October 1956, when full-scale rebellion broke out. The people rallied to the side of courageous Freedom Fighters against the Russian puppet leaders and after days of fierce

. the British cartoonist Leslie G. Illingworth expresses the world's horror at Soviet savagery unloosed on a defenseless Hungary

In East Berlin rioting, *courageous youths fight Soviet tanks with rocks*

... At Budapest

fighting, it seemed they had won. As thousands cheered, hundreds of Soviet tanks left Budapest and Russian Defense Minister Georgi Zhukov began negotiating with the free regime for complete withdrawal of Russian troops from Hungary. Then, in one of the greatest pieces of treachery in modern history, the Russian forces wheeled around and attacked Budapest. Fighting with a few tanks, rifles, and Molotov cocktails against Red armored divisions, the Freedom Fighters were doomed. It was massacre. As a sickened world listened, the rebel radio broadcast its last message: "Goodbye friends. Save our souls." Then began the pitiful trek of the defeated anti-Communists across a wintry land to refuge in Austria. The Kremlin had regained a satellite, but had been branded barbaric.

*A **new German Army** strengthened the Free World forces in Europe as the West strove to contain the Communists*

*A **Polaris missile** leaps from the water*

*First **Polaris-firing** nuclear submarine, U.S.S. George Washington*

Russian brutality in Budapest stiffened the resolve of the free world to strengthen its deterrent force, to make even surer that the Red leaders would think twice before turning an aggressive flood on other nations. Each year, the United States spent billions on military "hardware" and stepped-up technology which produced more and more destructive weapons like the Intercontinental Ballistic Missile, which could be fired thousands of miles, and the Polaris missile, which could be fired from atomic-powered submarines. To strengthen NATO, West Germany was allowed to rearm and soon organized the most respected military force in Europe. But in the end, effective defense would rest on effective leadership, and in the spring of 1958, the powerful voice of Gen. Charles de Gaulle was raised again. The austere, eloquent leader of the Free French in World War II had resigned in disgust as President of the postwar provisional government. The new French constitution failed to give any real power to the President. For twelve years, de Gaulle had waited while nineteen ministries of France were toppled and the economy was bled white by war in Indochina and Algeria. Finally, the Algerian rebellion forced France herself to the brink of civil war.

As the only man who could unite the people, de Gaulle was given almost dictatorial powers. His mission was to restore France as a first-class power. In his quest, he strengthened the economy and put France into the "atomic bomb club." But Algeria produced ever-recurring crises—whether her status was to be free outright, or free with ties to France. Algeria's 1,250,000 French residents caused de Gaulle more headaches than 9,000,000 Algerians. France regained prestige, but her great province in North Africa was too hot to handle.

Gen. Charles de Gaulle *returned to power after twelve years*

247

President Eisenhower *greets Premier Khrushchev on the Soviet leader's first visit to the United States*

Russia's angry attacks on the West were as steady as drum-beats and Nikita Khrushchev was a man of many faces and voices. In one breath, the tough, shrewd Ukrainian miner would blandly talk peace; in the next, he would boast, "We will bury you." On a visit to the United States in 1959, Khrushchev held several cordial talks with President Eisenhower. This mood led England's Prime Minister Harold Macmillan to press for a "summit" meeting in Paris, but Khrushchev wrecked the conference before it began. His excuse was the downing of an American reconnaissance plane while flying over Soviet territory. As Khrushchev and the West wrangled, a leader was rising who might make all their quarrels seem small, indeed. At the head of his 650 million people, Mao Tse-tung threatened to overshadow Russia's leaders as the prophet of Communism. The terrible strength of Mao's China was something Khrushchev, as well as the West, would have to reckon with.

Britain's *Prime Minister Harold Macmillan*

Communist Chinese *display a portrait of their leader, Mao Tse-tung, during a May Day parade in Peking*

Under the Red Heel in Asia

China *enters the rocket race*

Under the hard knuckles of Mao Tse-tung, China attempted "the great leap forward"—an ambitious program designed to modernize the ancient country. Leaning heavily on Soviet experience and assistance, Mao began the socialization of industry and the collectivization of the land. The familiar apparatus of totalitarianism appeared—mass arrests and executions, secret police, censorship, and party purges. In addition, Mao ruthlessly forced millions of Chinese into slave labor communes—breaking up traditional family units in order to produce more food and goods for the hugely-expanding population. Exploiting Chinese wealth and limitless manpower (photo, opposite page), the Red rulers bludgeoned China into the industrial age. Communism exacted a terrible price in human suffering—Mao's killings were estimated to number as high as 18 million. And these dead did not include the masses who starved. Despite massive internal problems posed by 650 million Chinese, Mao looked toward other lands and coveted them.

Chinese cotton mill workers carted off to the countryside to assist a 'people's commune' in harvesting the crops

Communist China was a land of huge armies, of vast manpower to spare. China showed her willingness to go to war by intervening against United Nations forces in Korea and sending arms to the Reds in Indochina. Chinese troops had pounced upon neighboring Tibet, driven out the spiritual leaders, and turned the Himalayas into a bloody battlefield. Next, China tested India, violating her borders. In Southeast Asia, China supplied the Communist guerrillas who harassed the newly-formed free governments. Though China had no navy to speak of, her air force contained an impressive number of jet planes, and the army, larger than any other on earth, was used for everything from attacking defenseless Tibet to harvesting rice in the communes.

Throughout the world, Red China sent arms and agents: In strife-torn Algeria, China gave the rebels some $10 million in aid; technicians were sent to Guinea and other nations in Africa; in Latin America, students were recruited for Peking's school for Communists. Even Russia became alarmed at Red China's belligerence, withdrew her technicians and withheld atomic information. For sooner or later, China was bound to develop a nuclear weapon, and when a power which had proved so heedless of human life obtained an atomic capability, the world faced even greater danger of a conflagration.

LEGEND

Armed aggression or strong political pressure by Red China for expansion

Economic penetration by Red China

Soviet Union sphere of influence

MANUFACTURING CENTERS

STEEL

COAL

OIL

HYDROELECTRIC STATIONS

ALUMINUM

TIN

TUNGSTEN

COPPER

LEAD & ZINC

ANTIMONY

RAILROADS

RAILROADS UNDER CONSTRUCTION

Fidel Castro *fanned hatred and resentment against America*

Jubilant *Cuban rebel soldiers . .*

'Pirate' of a Revolution

Long shaken by minor revolutions, the tempestuous nations that border the Caribbean Sea were jolted by a new and dangerous force—Communist infiltration. The most dramatic example came in Cuba, after Fidel Castro overthrew the dictatorship of Fulgencio Batista. Starting with twelve men, he carried on guerrilla warfare in the mountains, finally ousting Batista on Jan. 1, 1959. The United States' glowing hopes for a democratic regime were soon shattered as Castro failed to fulfill his promises and instead embarked on a calculated, Communist-inspired campaign against America, which finally led to severing diplomatic relations between the countries. Castro then began to export his brand of social revolution throughout Latin America; his diplomats and agents preached the revolutionary word everywhere they went. "Fidelism" thus spread chaos in troubled countries—Haiti, Panama, Guatemala, Venezuela, and the long-suffering Dominican Republic where dictator Rafael Trujillo ruled. And most of the Latin lands—where the masses had always been hungry and discontented—were fertile ground for the seeds of Communist propaganda.

. triumphantly wave a '26th of July' banner, the revolutionary battle-cry

Rafael Trujillo, the Dominican dictator

THE TURBULENT CARIBBEAN

Areas of political
unrest or open revolt

Areas of strong
communist penetration

Major U.S. bases

UNITED
STATES

Miami

BAHAMA

Nassau

ISLANDS
(British)

A T L A N T I C

Turks &
Caicos Is.
(British)

Havana

C U B A

Guantánamo

Revolutionary government of Fidel
established Jan. 1, 1959. Communist
and pro-Soviet policy 1960.

Jamaica
(W. I. F.)
Kingston

HAITI
Port-au-Prince

DOMINICAN
REPUBLIC
Ciudad
Trujillo

San Juan
PUERTO RICO
(U. S.)

VIRGIN IS.
(U. S. & Brit.)

O C E A N

Political unrest and threats of Cuban
intervention plague Haiti and the Trujillo
dictatorship in the Dominican Republic.

Antigua

Guadeloupe
(French)

WEST

Dominica

Martinique
(French)

INDIES

St. Lucia

Barbados

FED.
(British)

Grenada

C A R I B B E A N   S E A

NETH.
ANTILLES

Anti U. S. demonstrations
and movement to gain control
of Panama Canal 1959-60.

Lake
Maracaibo

Caracas

Port of
Spain
Trinidad
(W.I.F.)

CANAL
ZONE
(U. S.)

P A N A M A

Panama

V E N E Z U E L A

C O L O M B I A

BRITISH
GUIANA

0   100   200   300   400   500
Scale of Miles

Alarmed at Communist inroads in Latin America, the United States revived the "good neighbor" policy: President Eisenhower and Vice President Nixon made good-will tours, and economic programs were whipped into shape to contain "Fidelism." But the Soviet Union, too, was busy. Khrushchev was quick to lend support to Castro, thereby increasing Communist domination of a country only 90 miles from the United States. Farther south, Castro's influence waned; but though most South American nations had not been tainted by Red Cuba's Marxism, they were still plagued by chronic troubles—inflation, poverty, and underdevelopment. It was the United States' heavy task to keep Latin America from going the way of Cuba, for the West would need the friendship of Latin America, and it would have to make a powerful effort to win.

President Eisenhower *waves to crowds in Rio de Janeiro*

Premier Khrushchev *playfully grabbed Cuba's Castro in a Russian bear hug when they met at the United Nations*

SOUTH AMERICA
A Continent In-Between

Maracaibo • Caracas

VENEZUELA

BRITISH GUIANA

SURINAM

FRENCH GUIANA

COLOMBIA

Medellín
• Bogotá

Quito

ECUADOR

Belém

Amazon River

Manaus

P E R U

B R A Z I L

Recife

Lima

Salvador

La Paz

• Brasília

BOLIVIA

PARAGUAY

Rio de Janeiro

São Paulo

Asunción

Pôrto Alegre

C H I L E

A R G E N T I N A

Córdoba

Rosario

URUGUAY

Santiago

Buenos Aires

Montevideo

CAPE HORN

LEGEND

Areas of concentrated settlement and extensive economic development

Lightly populated areas of slight economic development

Primitive or backward areas

Cities over 2,000,000 population

Cities over 500,000 population

Scale of Miles

0   200   400   600   800   1000

© C.S. Hammond & Co.

Out of Colonialism, a New Africa

Nowhere on earth did the flood tide of nationalism wash over the land so dramatically as in Africa. Nearly every year after World War II, new flags were unfurled across the continent and European ensigns hauled down. The once-mighty French Empire virtually came to an end. Britain, too, granted some of her colonies independence and started others on the road to self-government. And the Belgian Empire lost a domain with the formation of the Republic of the Congo. In many cases, movements for independence—and independence itself—brought riot and strife. In the Congo, native leaders—untrained, undisciplined, and unaware of the burdens of responsibility—brought the nation perilously close to anarchy. To power-drunk citizens of the new republic, an African newspaper soberly warned: "Freedom is not a golden paradise of money, beer, and idleness." Other parts of Africa were seared by dissension, too. In Algeria, the land was torn by rebellion; in South Africa, ground down by a harsh white-supremacy policy, the native populace seemed like an unexploded time bomb. Some governments, however—notably Nigeria and Ghana—made the transition from colonial status to independence with peace and dignity. Their experience showed that given careful training, the black African could move toward responsible, representative, and workable government. And it was on such unruffled transitions Africa's future rested, for unless her peoples could master the complicated and unfamiliar techniques of self-government, Africa could break up in a fiery, Balkanized continent of hate.

In South Africa, a grim and ominous paradox. Whites bowl on manicured greens . . .

. . . and in the crowded native slums, white policemen break up Negro demonstrations

In the Congo, *even children were caught in the senseless strife that came with freedom from Belgium . . .*

. . . smiling Nigerians, in contrast, applauded the joining of their new nation to the British Commonwealth

COLONIAL AFRICA 1939

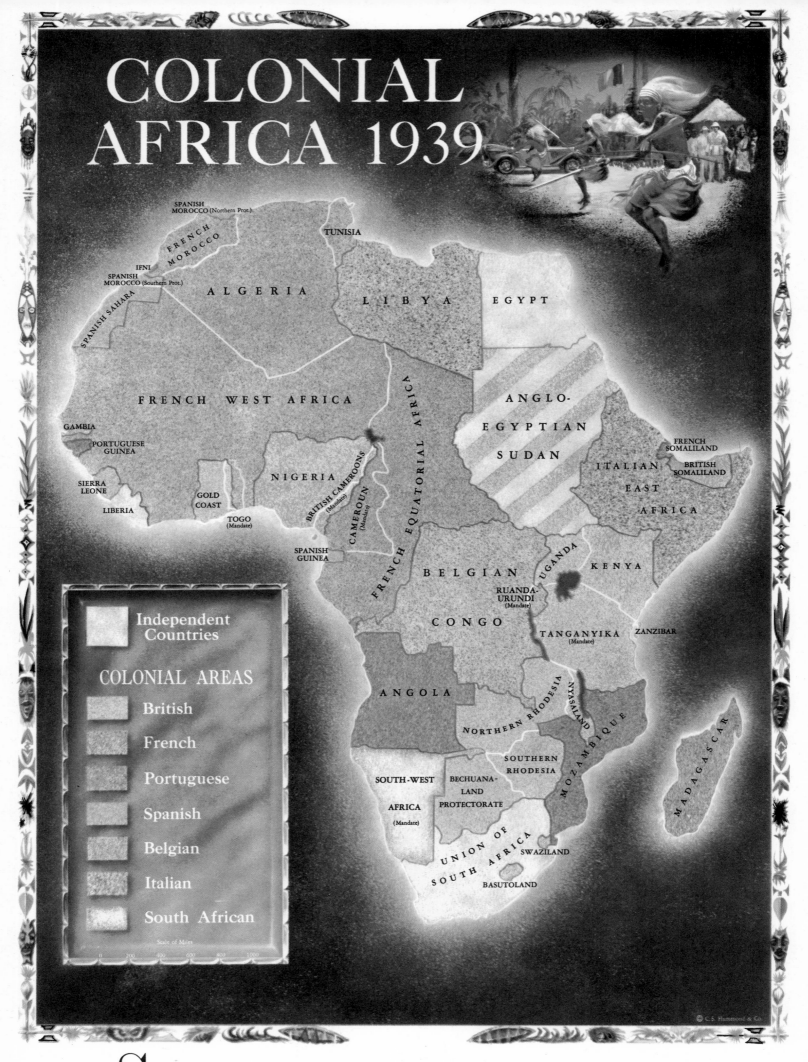

SPANISH MOROCCO (Northern Prot.)

FRENCH MOROCCO

TUNISIA

IFNI

SPANISH MOROCCO (Southern Prot.)

ALGERIA

LIBYA

EGYPT

SPANISH SAHARA

FRENCH WEST AFRICA

ANGLO-EGYPTIAN SUDAN

GAMBIA

PORTUGUESE GUINEA

FRENCH SOMALILAND

ITALIAN EAST AFRICA

BRITISH SOMALILAND

SIERRA LEONE

NIGERIA

LIBERIA

GOLD COAST

TOGO (Mandate)

BRITISH CAMEROONS (Mandate)

CAMEROUN (Mandate)

FRENCH EQUATORIAL AFRICA

SPANISH GUINEA

BELGIAN

UGANDA

KENYA

RUANDA-URUNDI (Mandate)

CONGO

TANGANYIKA (Mandate)

ZANZIBAR

ANGOLA

NORTHERN RHODESIA

NYASALAND

MOZAMBIQUE

MADAGASCAR

SOUTHERN RHODESIA

SOUTH-WEST AFRICA (Mandate)

BECHUANA-LAND PROTECTORATE

UNION OF SOUTH AFRICA

SWAZILAND

BASUTOLAND

Independent Countries

COLONIAL AREAS

British

French

Portuguese

Spanish

Belgian

Italian

South African

Scale of Miles

0   200   400   600   800   1000

© C. S. Hammond & Co.

Seeking Africa's riches, the industrial powers of Europe cut up the continent among themselves. In 1939, there were only three independent nations remaining: Liberia, South Africa, and Egypt.

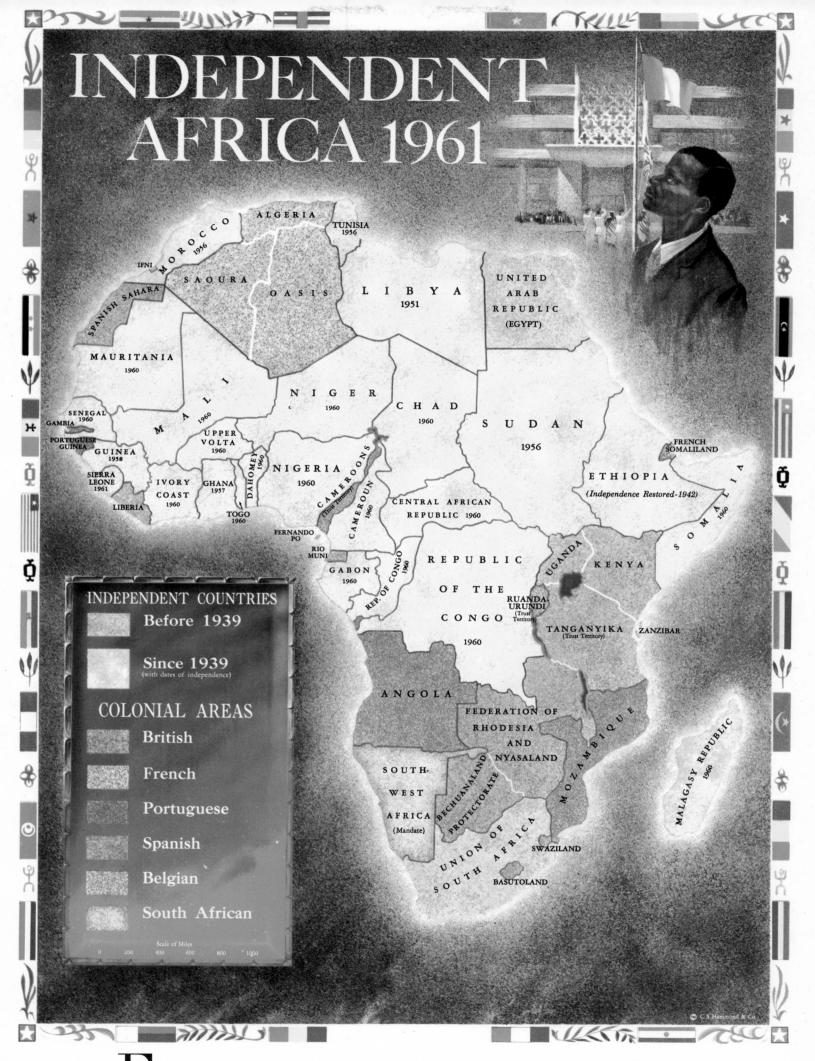

INDEPENDENT AFRICA 1961

INDEPENDENT COUNTRIES

- Before 1939
- Since 1939 (with dates of independence)

COLONIAL AREAS

- British
- French
- Portuguese
- Spanish
- Belgian
- South African

Scale of Miles
0   200   400   600   800   1000

MOROCCO 1956
IFNI
ALGERIA
TUNISIA 1956
SPANISH SAHARA
SAOURA
OASIS
LIBYA 1951
UNITED ARAB REPUBLIC (EGYPT)
MAURITANIA 1960
MALI 1960
NIGER 1960
CHAD 1960
SUDAN 1956
FRENCH SOMALILAND
SENEGAL 1960
GAMBIA
PORTUGUESE GUINEA
GUINEA 1958
UPPER VOLTA 1960
ETHIOPIA (Independence Restored-1942)
SOMALIA 1960
SIERRA LEONE 1961
IVORY COAST 1960
GHANA 1957
DAHOMEY 1960
NIGERIA 1960
CAMEROONS (Trust Territory)
CENTRAL AFRICAN REPUBLIC 1960
LIBERIA
TOGO 1960
CAMEROUN 1960
FERNANDO PO
RIO MUNI
GABON 1960
REP. OF CONGO 1960
REPUBLIC OF THE CONGO 1960
UGANDA
KENYA
RUANDA-URUNDI (Trust Territory)
TANGANYIKA (Trust Territory)
ZANZIBAR
ANGOLA
FEDERATION OF RHODESIA AND NYASALAND
MOZAMBIQUE
MALAGASY REPUBLIC 1960
SOUTH-WEST AFRICA (Mandate)
BECHUANALAND PROTECTORATE
SWAZILAND
UNION OF SOUTH AFRICA
BASUTOLAND

© C.S. Hammond & Co

From World War II on, the irresistible pressures of nationalism toppled the great empires, breaking them up into many independent nations, each with its own flag, government, army, and problems.

United and Disunited

As the new nations emerged in Africa, the attention of the world turned as never before to that vast continent. Statesmen of great—and lesser—powers made pilgrimages to Africa to gain the good will of the new nations. The Soviet bloc sent skilled technicians and diplomats who attempted to influence the new governments for their own ends, or to fan the flames of rebellion against the few remaining colonial powers. The Western nations sought to combat Soviet influence—for however confusing the political situation in the new, unstable republics, the West simply could not let millions of Africans slip into Communism by default. The African humanitarian, Albert Schweitzer, summed up the challenge: "We are not free to choose whether or not we want to help the colored man. We simply must. And what good we do to him is not charity but reparation." The United Nations tried its best to keep Africa from erupting—nation against nation, tribe against tribe, black against white. And in the U.N. General Assembly, the voices of the newly independent nations were heard in the council chambers. As more and more of the new nations were admitted to membership, the balance of power shifted to the states of Asia and emergent Africa.

High up in the Atlas Mountains, an Algerian rebel stands guard

United Nations troops struggled hard to pacify the violent Congo

262

In the U.N. General Assembly, *the new Ivory Coast delegation is seated—another member of the new, powerful African bloc*

Diplomats *from the Soviet Union woo the new delegates of Senegal*

Delegates *from Asia symbolize a new U.N. power*

The surging, sometimes irrational, forces of nationalism sorely tried the United Nations as the '60s began. In hot spots like the Congo, the U.N. was hampered not only by the jealous, quarreling native factions, but by the surreptitious tactics of Communist nations who fostered chaos and confusion, hoping to spread their dismal creed. In the General Assembly, the Soviet Union, citing the rising number of African and Asian states, demanded that the United Nations be reorganized. The West could ill afford to allow Russia to revamp the U.N. structure to suit Soviet ends. On paper, at least, an absolute majority in the General Assembly could be mustered from 50-odd nations having less total population than the United States alone. No one would deny the new African and Asian nations their due; yet it was in no one's interest to let the brand-new republics dominate the proceedings. Some kind of readjustment was inevitable if the organization was to pursue its lofty but arduous goal of world peace. In spite of all the pitfalls, and for all its shortcomings, the U.N. had proven its worth in Korea, Israel, Suez, and the Congo. And in the decade of the '60s, mankind looked hopefully to the delegates of many colors gathered at the U.N. to somehow solve the crucial problems of a changing world in the nuclear age, and the problems that were surely coming as man moved to break his tethers to earth.

Facing the U.N., these noble words from Isaiah

Gazing spaceward, *this astronaut symbolizes man's adventure beyond the Earth*

The World of Space

Above the disorderly earthly scene of power politics, Cold War and revolution, lies another world, serene, timeless—the world of space. There, in the velvet black realm, the restless spirit of man faced its greatest challenge as the seventh decade of the twentieth century began. On the planet Earth, the last physical frontiers had been crossed: The Everests scaled, the Antarctic wastes charted, the deepest deep of the ocean plumbed. There remained but one direction for man to go in his unending search for adventure and understanding: Outward into space, onward to the moon and the planets and then beyond to alien worlds revolving around sister suns.

To break free of his terrestrial bonds and soar free, to comprehend the grand design of the universe—these are ancient aspirations of mankind, expressed in such myths as that of the Greek artificer Icarus and in the insights of the Greek geometer Pythagoras. Yet, for centuries, man could only dream—and calculate. Copernicus, Kepler, Newton, and Einstein helped create a new view of the cosmos. Their picture was supplemented by what the astronomers' telescopic eyes and ears reported. Meanwhile, the soaring imaginations of a da Vinci and a Verne provided fuel for latter-day voyagers. Then, with the development of giant rockets spurred on by World War II, the Verneian fiction could be turned into reality. First, man sent out his robot satellites: Sputniks and Explorers to scout the new world and radio back their findings. Next came short trips into space by monkeys, mice, and dogs. But the incandescent moment, the time when the dream of Icarus was realized, belonged to man alone. Buoyant, exultant, triumphant, the first man in space could survey a new domain. Above him were the unwinking stars in their true red, white and yellow colors. Below, the home planet Earth, a glowing sphere suffused with blue.

*A **great** island of stars in the sea of space, our Milky Way would look like this from Andromeda galaxy*

to moon .... 1.3 *light seconds*

to sun .... 8 *light minutes*

to nearest star .... 4.3 *light years*

to center of Milky Way .... 30,000 *light years*

to nearest galaxy .... 170,000 *light years*

to edge of observed universe ... 6,000,000,000 *light years*

marks the position in which our sun would appear in a rendering of our "home" Milky Way galaxy. Photo above is of Andromeda, twin of the Milky Way. Dotted line traces distance to galaxy center. The Milky Way, made up of some 100 billion stars, is but one of millions of galaxies in the known universe. Palomar's telescope now brings in galaxies 6 billion light years* away—and still no end.

* Light travels at 186,300 miles per second. One light-year equals 6 trillion miles.

Some 5,000 years separate the first skywatchers, peering up along the banks of the Nile and Euphrates from the first astronauts, peering down through their periscopes at the blue planet Earth. Within this span, man has come to apprehend how insignificant, puny, and transitory his own world is. To the ancient sky observers, man appeared unique; his planet seemed the cynosure of the universe. Was Earth not the central, stationary platform over which the celestial bodies performed for his benefit? Now, man's vision has changed. He realizes how fleeting is his history in time—the five millenniums of civilization but a brief moment in the grand design of the universe.

Today, he realizes his true place in the universe— one of a thousand forms of life on the crust of a small planet that circles a minor sun on the edge of a 100-billion-starred galaxy called the Milky Way. And this galaxy, in turn, is only one among a billion in the known universe. Yet, paradoxically, his sense of uniqueness has been enhanced rather than destroyed. No longer does he peer upward solely in wonderment and worship. Now his mind comprehends cosmic relationships far more exhilarating than the notion that Earth is the center of the universe. But this wisdom came slowly, in spurts—after many false starts in the effort to understand.

In Greek mythology, *Icarus, wings unstuck, fell into the sea*

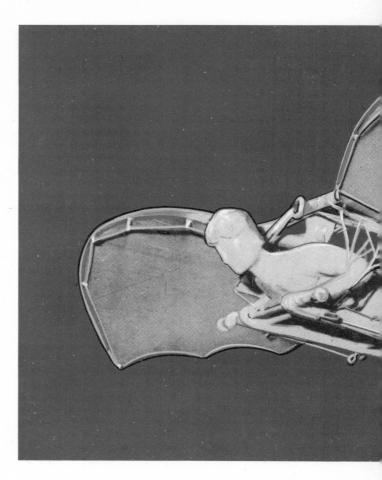

Italy's da Vinci *outdid Icarus with his Ornithopter*

A medieval traveler *inspects the world as he knew it—flat Earth, vaulted sky, cloud-driven stars*

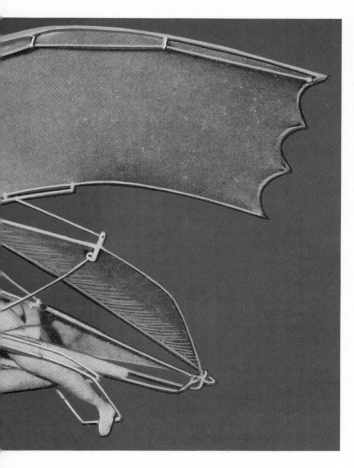

the pilot's own foot power was to operate the wings

Flying moonmen *brought astronomer Herschel's dreamboat home*

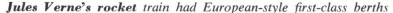

Jules Verne's rocket *train had European-style first-class berths*

Dreams of Wings

In man's efforts to conquer space, his imagination has always run ahead of his accomplishments and understanding. The first astronauts—the archetypes and symbol of human aspirations—were Icarus and his father Daedalus in the myths of the Greeks. In a bold but fatal voyage, father and son fashioned goose-feather wings and fastened them with wax to their bodies. But Icarus flew so near the sun that the wax melted and he fell into the sea. Centuries later the Italian Leonardo da Vinci applied his sublime genius to human flight. His solution was the Ornithopter, or foot-operated flying machine—a wooden frame, huge cloth wings, a windlass, and a series of ropes and pulleys. Da Vinci's creation never got off the ground; but nothing could deter the vision of nineteenth century dreamers like England's Sir John Herschel and France's Jules Verne. Herschel speculated that the moon was inhabited by a winged race. Author Verne sent rocket trains to the moon in his 1865 novel *From the Earth to the Moon.* For his launching spot he chose a site in central Florida—only 120 miles from the space-age jumping off point at Cape Canaveral.

Ptolemy held that Earth was the fixed center of the universe

Galileo (pointing) was a brilliant theorist .

Copernicus displayed his model of Earth moving around the sun

Not all men dreamed of space; some tried to understand it. In sixth-century B.C. Greece, Pythagoras concluded on the basis of his geometry that Earth, for all its seeming flatness, was really a sphere. These insights were obscured by the ludicrous teachings of the Egyptian Ptolemy, who in the second century A.D. set forth Earth-centered theories of the universe which were to dominate astronomy for fourteen centuries. Then, the fresh winds of the Renaissance swept away the old ideas. In 1543, a Pole named Nicholas Copernicus contradicted Ptolemy and the lessons of the senses when he declared that the sun, not Earth, was the center of the universe—and offered mathematical explanations of planetary motions. The walls of orthodoxy had been breached. With the invention of the telescope in the

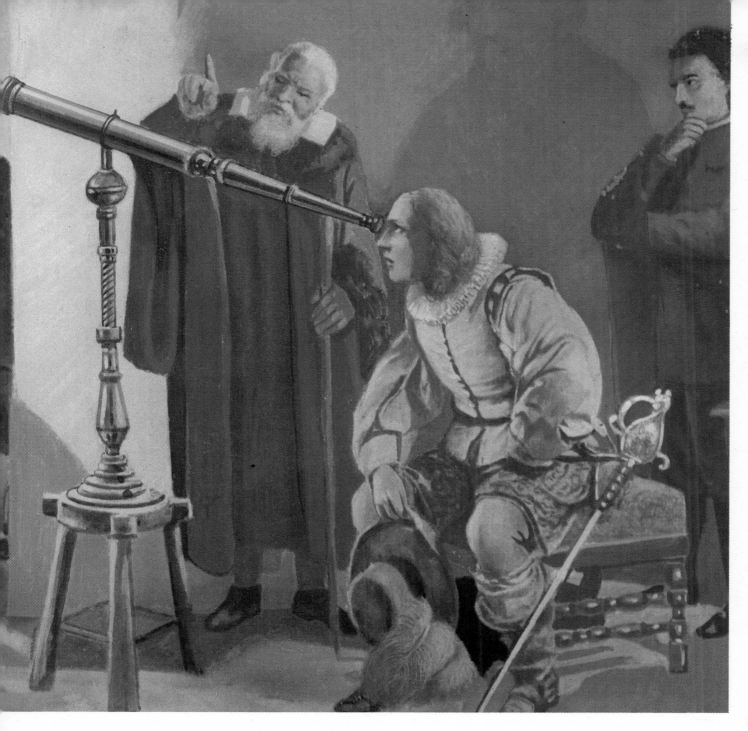

, and also knew how to promote his ideas

The chief architect *of new view was Sir Isaac Newton*

seventeenth century, the rebuilding job begun by Copernicus could be completed. When the Italian Galileo Galilei (1564-1642) looked out into space with his homemade telescope, he discovered planets with three dimensions and characteristics of their own—not mere dim lights hung in a vaulted sky. Then the German Johannes Kepler, in 1609, showed that the planets moved in elliptical rather than circular orbits. With Sir Isaac Newton's monumental formulations 77 years later, the new astronomical view was firmly established. By combining the insights of men like Galileo and Kepler, Newton was able to set forth a universal theory of gravitation. With his three famous general laws of motion it became possible to determine the paths of all bodies in the fixed frame of space.

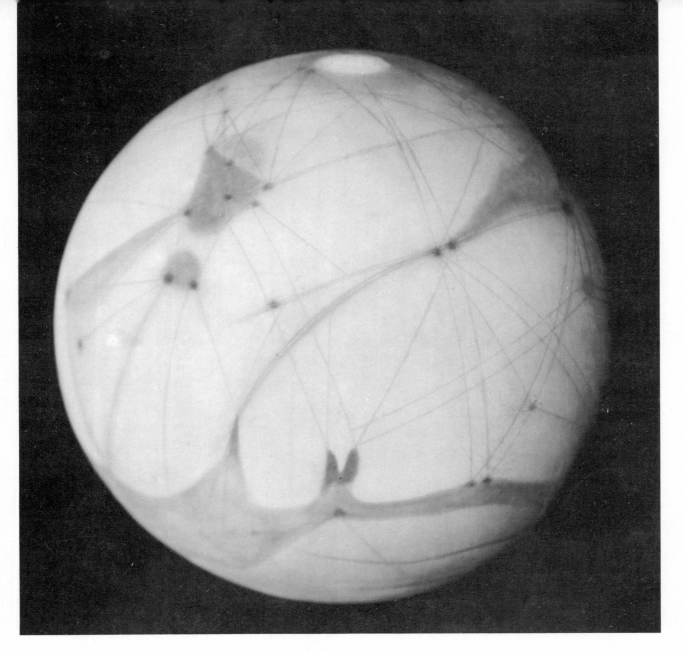

Heated debate *over existence of life on Mars began when nineteenth-century observers claimed to see 'canals'*

Harvard's *Percival Lowell was pro-canal*

Chicago's *Prof. A.A. Michelson set the stage for Einstein*

For three centuries, Newton's view of the cosmos fitted the observed facts of nature. Then, in a classic experiment performed in 1881, the American physicists A.A. Michelson and E.W. Morley measured the speed of light and found that one of the main pillars of Newtonian thought no longer was tenable. Something had to give. The break came in 1905 when a 26-year-old mathematician named Albert Einstein enunciated his Special Theory of Relativity and then followed with the comprehensive General Theory in 1915. Einstein's new views of space, time, and the universe, so staggering to the non-mathematician, were dramatically verified by experiment. But the final, cosmic answer—the grand and unifying explanation of the universe—eluded Einstein, and still eludes man.

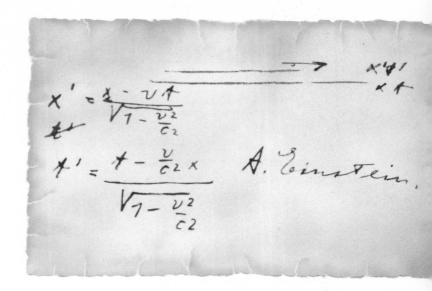

Hair rumpled, casually dressed, Einstein was a celebrity in a world where few could grasp his ideas

275

Charting the Outward Regions

The universe that Newton and Einstein sought to explain stretches mysteriously across the night skies. On a clear night, there are some 5,000 heavenly bodies visible to the naked eye. Early telescopes disclosed more than two million stars. Since then, bigger and better telescopes have plumbed unimagined regions in space. The world's biggest optical "eye," the 200-inch Hale telescope at Palomar Observatory has encompassed the light of billions of stars. Astronomers now know these are not merely pinpoints of light but gasses whose temperatures determine their jewel-like colors. Spectroscopes attached to telescopic lenses can analyze this starlight to determine the stars' chemical composition. Thanks to nuclear chemistry and physics, the modern astronomer can relate the luminosity and position of the stars to the origin, age, and evolution of the universe. The star luminaries, we now know, are in various stages of evolution: Some are expanding red giants in the prime of development, others are extinct white dwarfs. By looking out into space to the limits of Palomar's range, astronomers are actually looking at starlight that started toward Earth six billion years ago. Thus astronomers can probe the dimensions of time as well as the depths of space, and cosmologists are not without clues to the cosmic design that Einstein and others sought. They suggest, based on mathematical calculations of the luminosity, or power output, of certain star clusters, that the universe is 15 billion years old. They know, as well, that it is expanding—that the giant galaxies are rushing away from each other like inelastic spots on an inflating balloon.

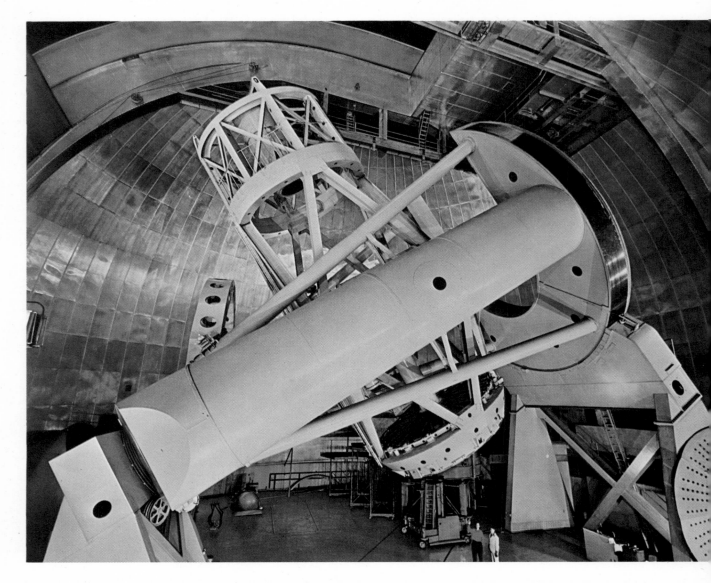

Close-up *of 200-inch eye shows lens at bottom of birdcage telescope tube*

Moonlight burnishes the shutters on dome of the Hale telescope on Mount Palomar in California

Gaseous mass *known as the crab nebula (for its shape) was a supernova—titanic explosion signaling the death of a star*

Smoke ring *of gas circles star in later evolution stage*

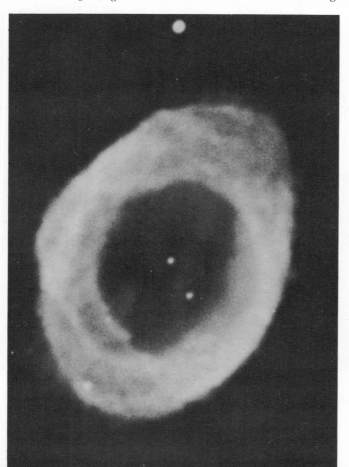

Cell, animal, man, star, galaxy, universe—on every level that science investigates there is the same pattern of evolution. In the beginning, according to one new theory, there were magnetized cosmic clouds. (Some of this suspected raw material of creation is shown on these two pages.) From this primeval gas and dust, the Milky Way galaxy was formed; perhaps other galaxies are now being formed in the same way. Cosmologists Thomas Gold, Fred Hoyle and Hermann Bondi hold that as the expanding galaxies rush outward they leave behind trails of hydrogen atoms which become the stuff of new stars. This is the theory of the "Steady State": Galaxies are born and die while the universe itself remains a constant through infinity—no beginning, no ending. New findings, however, may upset the Steady State theory. Palomar's Allan Sandage has found that the galactic expansion rate is slowing. According to competing cosmologies, a contraction of the universe may come 100 billion years hence.

Cold cloud *of gas and opaque dust squeezed by hot surrounding gas which lights it from behind forms the Horsehead nebula*

Whirlpool galaxy *shows distinct spiral structure. Astronomers now are trying to fit galaxies into coherent age pattern*

French hot-air balloons had a certain hauteur. *This one reached the giddy height of 1,500 feet*

Flight—and Onward Into Rocketry

The vehicle that ultimately was to lift man towards the stars his telescopes so tantalizingly disclosed had quite humble origins. During the Mongol siege of the city of Kaifeng in the Chinese province of Honan, one side—no one is sure which one—employed "arrows of flaming fire." The date was 1232 A.D. The rocket, a self-propelled "arrow" that carried its own fuel supply, was born. The Mongols (or the Chinese) had harnessed without knowing it the force implicit in Newton's third law of motion: For every action there is an equal and opposite reaction. Anyone who has ever stepped vigorously—and thoughtlessly—out of a rowboat knows how this action-reaction works. The idea is the same in a rocket; as the incendiary mixture burns and jets rearward, it thrusts the rocket forward.

According to legend, the first to test this rocket principle in a theoretically airborne vehicle was a Chinese Emperor Wan-hoo (circa 1500). Wan-hoo's plan was to hold two kites in his hands and strap himself to a chair with 47 powder rockets attached. Then, 47 torch-carrying coolies were to rush the machine and ignite the rockets. The technique worked—too well. Chairborne Wan-hoo and his rockets went up in flames. In 1783, the Montgolfier brothers made the first successful manned flight—a ten-minute ascent in their colorful hot-air balloon. Advanced versions had exhaust holes poked in the sides so the hot air could escape and provide directional thrust. But these jet balloons went the way of Wan-hoo.

Wan-hoo's chairborne rocket had one thing to commend it. It was simple

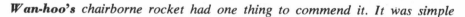

A prophet without honor, Robert Goddard stands next to his rocket on day of historic flight at Aunt Effie's farm

Russia had a Goddard, too—his name was Prof. Konstantin Tsiolkovsky, space dreamer and practical tinkerer as well

A variety of inventors tinkered with the notion of reaction flight in the decades after the French balloonists, but it remained for a quiet, mustached, American physicist named Robert H. Goddard to get the idea off the ground. In the 1920s, the neighbors around his Aunt Effie Ward's farm outside Worcester, Mass., considered Goddard and his ungainly contraption rather foolish. They chided him with the nickname "Moony."

By today's standards, Goddard's 10-foot-long rocket was indeed quaint. The combustion chamber, about the size of a Fourth of July rocket, was on the top; the propellant tanks were slung below—the reverse of today's designs. Thin pipes connected the two, feeding liquid oxygen and gasoline into the chamber. But on March 16, 1926, at Aunt Effie's farm, the glorious payoff was achieved. Henry Sachs, Goddard's assistant, ignited the primitive motor with a blowtorch tied to the end of a long pole. The rocket soared 41 feet high, veered to the left, and smashed into a slushy cabbage patch. With Yankee frugality, Goddard and his wife picked up the pieces. The flight was a milestone—Goddard had launched the world's first liquid-fueled rocket. But a jazz-happy and speculation-bent society missed the significance of his achievement. Even the "experts" were wide of the mark. For example, the New York Times headlined a story of Professor Goddard's activities "A Severe Strain on Credulity." Goddard became even more retiring, and continued to work alone. On the eve of World War II, when he urged a United States military board to begin a missile program, he was told: "The next war will be fought with the trench mortar."

Traveling *faster than the sound of its motors, the V-2 was an eerie and formidable weapon*

Rocketeer *von Braun today, still the visionary*

In Germany, however, during the roaring '20s, there was a group of rocket bugs who paid attention to Goddard's pioneering work. One of them was a blond, bulky youngster of Junker stock named Wernher von Braun. He and his companions used gas-soaked rags and a long reach to light their finicky rockets. Fuel and materials were wangled from industrialists with the promise that they would be let in on the ground floor of space flight. For a launch site the youngsters talked the Berlin city fathers into giving them free lease to an abandoned ammunition storage area. Von Braun and his daredevil companions were primarily interested in space flight to the moon, but another group watched with more worldly vision. German Army Capt. Walter Dornberger reasoned that rocketry offered an approach to long-range weapons unhampered by the disarmament terms of the Versailles Treaty. In 1932, at the age of 20, von Braun went to work for the German Army. Through the 1930s, the Germans worked in secret, largely left alone because Hitler had dreamed that rockets would never reach England.

Von Braun aimed at the stars, but the first V-2s sent a ton of TNT across the English Channel

Hitler's dream that a rocket would never fly was only one of the barriers to the Dornberger-von Braun plans. There were wartime manpower squeezes, British air raids. Above all, there were technical problems like making valves to handle fuels at just the right mixture and designing ingenious vanes to steer the rocket. Finally, on a cloudless day early in October 1942, a cigar-shaped 13.5-ton monster, painted with black and white stripes for tracking purposes, lifted into the North German skies at Peenemünde. It rose 60 miles and dropped into the sea. That day Dorn-berger could claim the space ship was born. Hitler revoked his dream. The rocket became Vengeance Weapon No. 2, the V-2. On the evening of Sept. 8, 1944, at 6:43, just about the time the London bus queues were longest, the first combat V-2 fell on Chiswick. Some 16 seconds later, a second hit Epping. "We hit the wrong planet," von Braun later declared. Unfortunately for the Germans, the V-2 had joined up too late and in too little numbers. Had it been ready six months earlier, General Eisenhower was to write, the invasion of Europe might have failed.

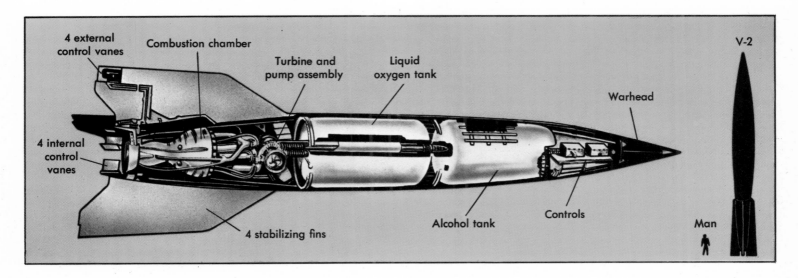

4 external control vanes
Combustion chamber
Turbine and pump assembly
Liquid oxygen tank
Warhead
V-2
4 internal control vanes
4 stabilizing fins
Alcohol tank
Controls
Man

Convair's 774 was first of big
American postwar liquid rockets

Wac-Corporal, a V-2 with tiny
American rocket, set altitude mark

Martin's Viking explored upper
atmosphere at White Sands, N.M.

The Russians drew an early bead on space, as this 1959 photo of nose-cone recovery shows

To the victors of World War II went the spoils. The advancing Russians seized Peenemünde, its rockets, and perhaps 3,000 technicians. But von Braun and 120 of his top men escaped and surrendered to the West. As "wards" of the American Army, they were eventually brought to White Sands Proving Grounds in New Mexico to fire off the handful of V-2s whisked away from the Russians. Despite some successes, von Braun's team languished. Missiles were judged too costly for the austerity budgets of the late 1940s. But in Russia, missiles and space flight were given a strong boost: The Red Army was put in charge of all rockets; the Soviet Academy of Sciences set the cosmic goal—to be first into space.

Artillery General A. A. Blagonravov had undivided command of Red Army rockets from the start

Sputnik—and Conquest

In Washington, D.C., on that first Friday in October 1957, Russian and American scientists had finished week-long talks on the International Geophysical Year, an unprecedented cooperative study of man's environment, and were unwinding at a Soviet Embassy reception. Then came the stunning, history-changing announcement from Moscow: The Soviet Union had sent a satellite into orbit around the Earth. At that moment, on Oct. 4, it was streaking across the skies 560 miles high (photo, right).

The world itself was swept into Sputnik I's orbit. The first giant step in the conquest of space had been made. American scientists, who naturally had expected their own satellite would be first up, congratulated their Russian colleagues. But the steady *beep beep beep* of Sputnik I's radio had an ominous tone. The first satellite, as an achievement of a despotic state committed to world dominance, signaled the extension of the Cold War to outer space—a fact that NEWSWEEK (below) recognized in its issue out four days afterward.

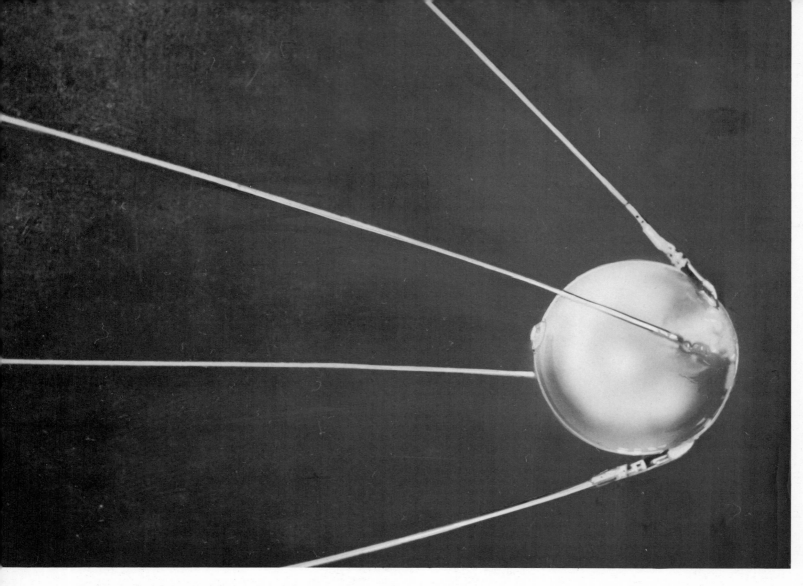

Polished aluminum sphere gleaming, four antennas rakishly angled, Russia's Sputnik I was first addition to the heavens

In this model of Sputnik II, Laika's porthole is seen at bottom; close-up shows feeding apparatus for first space traveler

That Russia—the backward giant that had industrialized so much later than the West—should be first into space was enough of a jolt. But when American rocketeers noted that the beachball-sized Sputnik I weighed in at 184 pounds, their concern was compounded. To put such a hefty object in orbit meant that Russian rockets apparently could generate twice the thrust of America's best space engines. The second jarring shock came less than a month later. On Nov. 2, 1957, a mongrel dog named Laika went into orbit in a sealed cabin complete with feeding tray and porthole. Sputnik II —dog, instruments and all—had an announced weight of 1,120 pounds, about the same as a Volkswagen car. Laika had only a limited oxygen supply, however, and the first living being in orbit perished after one week. Beneath the dizzying whirl of the sputniks, the spotlight of world attention shifted to Vanguard—America's answer to Sputnik weighed but 3.2 pounds. On Dec. 6 the count down reached its climax in the goldfish bowl of Cape Canaveral. The slim Vanguard rocket rose four feet, toppled over, and exploded ingloriously. It was a fizzle heard round the world. Now ideas and men long held in limbo were given the green light. From Washington the word was flashed to Armyman von Braun: "Let's go, Wernher." On Jan. 30, 1958, three months after his go-ahead, von Braun's team put the United States back in the space race—and made a key discovery the sputniks had overlooked.

Explorer I—*first American satellite*

'Firing Command'—*Jupiter-C rocket, carrying Explorer I, is committed to flight*

HOSTILE ENVIRONMENT

C

D

A

EARTH

VAN ALLEN RADIATION BELTS

OUTER

PROTONS ELECTRONS

INNER BELT

B

E

SECONDARY PARTICLES

B

F

A

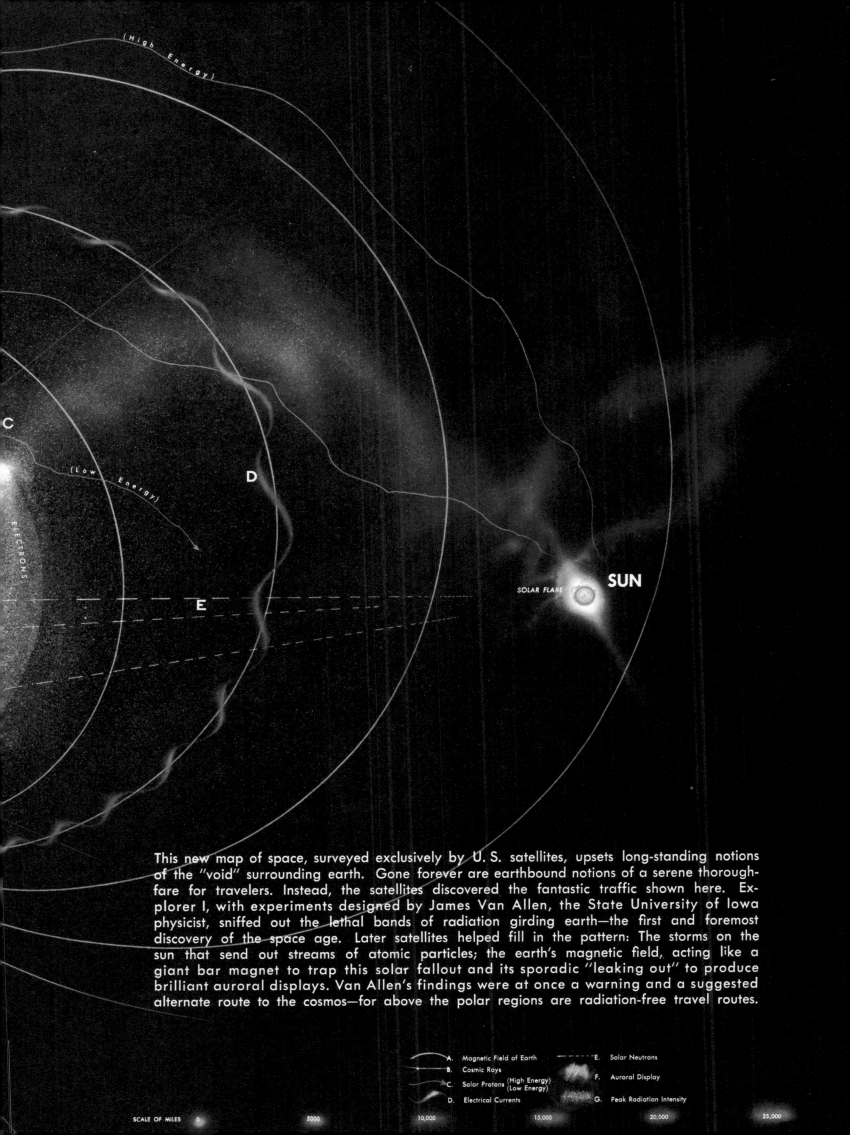

(High Energy)

C

(Low Energy)

ELECTRONS

D

E

SOLAR FLARE SUN

This new map of space, surveyed exclusively by U. S. satellites, upsets long-standing notions of the "void" surrounding earth. Gone forever are earthbound notions of a serene thorough-fare for travelers. Instead, the satellites discovered the fantastic traffic shown here. Explorer I, with experiments designed by James Van Allen, the State University of Iowa physicist, sniffed out the lethal bands of radiation girding earth—the first and foremost discovery of the space age. Later satellites helped fill in the pattern: The storms on the sun that send out streams of atomic particles; the earth's magnetic field, acting like a giant bar magnet to trap this solar fallout and its sporadic "leaking out" to produce brilliant auroral displays. Van Allen's findings were at once a warning and a suggested alternate route to the cosmos—for above the polar regions are radiation-free travel routes.

A. Magnetic Field of Earth   E. Solar Neutrons

B. Cosmic Rays

C. Solar Protons (High Energy)   F. Auroral Display
                   (Low Energy)

D. Electrical Currents   G. Peak Radiation Intensity

SCALE OF MILES   0   5000   10,000   15,000   20,000   25,000

The early Navy Transits carried a hitchhiking satellite

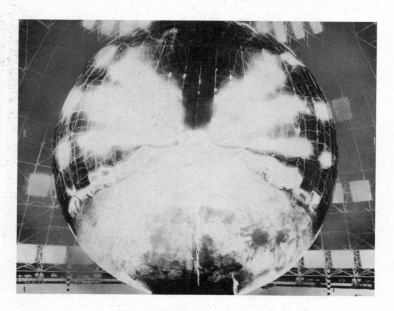

Echo's aluminum-plastic skin made a 100-foot-wide target

Courier I's message center handled 118 million words

The spectacular firsts of the early space age went to the Russians—first satellite, first animal in orbit, first satellite of the sun, first lunar bull's-eye, first photo of the moon's far side, first animals brought back alive from orbit. But the United States nonetheless could claim advantages in space both of quantity and of quality. Consider the statistics: In the three short years after the first Sputnik, man-made satellites became fixtures as unremarkable in the heavens as the moon and the stars. The two space powers sent 41 objects into orbit between 1958 and 1960; of these 33 were made-in-America.

While the satellites launched by the Russian rocketeers were much heavier, the American voyagers made up for the weight disadvantage by their cleverness—and their utility. These "sophisticated" satellites were devoted primarily to exploring the alien environment surrounding Earth, to demonstrating the practical uses of space —the direct payoffs to the public—and to paving the way for man's own voyage into space. (A sampling of these practical satellites is shown here and some of the space explorers and forerunners of manned flight appear on the following two pages.) There were, for example, the highly successful Echo and Courier communications satellites, both forerunners of space messenger

Midas detection system built to function by '63

systems. Echo, a giant aluminum balloon, served as a radio "mirror"—a reflector for telephone messages and photo relays. The solar cell-studded Courier, with its four transmitters and four FM receivers, could pick up, store, and deliver signals from one point on the earth to another. Another experimental system which promised everyday dividends was the Navy's navigation satellite series called Transit. With four Transit satellites in orbit broadcasting a signal, any properly equipped surface ship can get a "fix" on its precise position at sea.

A fix of another sort was to be provided by the Air Force's Midas series of satellites. Midas, an acronym for Missile Defense Alarm System, carries heat sensors to detect the exhaust plumes of hostile missiles the instant they blast up through the atmosphere. But the satellite which above all promised the most immediate benefits was the talented Tiros weather watcher. The first experimental Tiros demonstrated how a television camera orbiting 430 miles above Earth could take a good look at this planet's cloud cover and radio back information on 1,000-mile-wide storm systems. As Dr. Harry Wexler, the United States Weather Bureau's chief of research, put it: "These clouds are nature's own weather maps."

RCA scientist adjusts TV camera in this underside view of Tiros

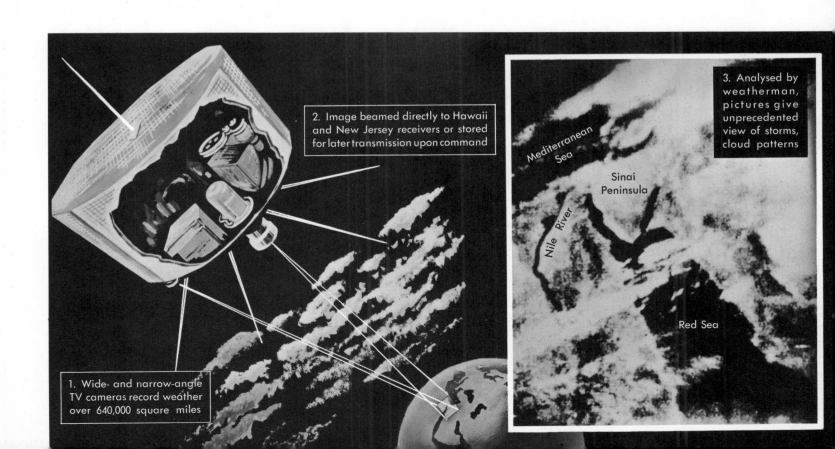

2. Image beamed directly to Hawaii and New Jersey receivers or stored for later transmission upon command

3. Analysed by weatherman, pictures give unprecedented view of storms, cloud patterns

Mediterranean Sea

Sinai Peninsula

Nile River

Red Sea

1. Wide- and narrow-angle TV cameras record weather over 640,000 square miles

Solving a Great Puzzle

"Space is radioactive," a young State University of Iowa physicist named Ernest Ray exclaimed somewhat inaccurately but graphically one spring day in 1958. Working under the direction of Iowa's James Van Allen, Ray had been replaying the tape of space radiation measurements made by recorders aboard the Explorer III satellite. Suddenly the counting rate went up with a *B-r-r-r-p-p* sound. Thus, the Van Allen Radiation Belts were discovered; and the first major piece in the puzzling map of space filled in. For the first time, man was beginning to understand the path that awaited him on his journey into the cosmos. Radiation, however, is but one of the barriers facing him. There must be some sort of two-way communication and there must be some reasonably certain assurance of returning. Pioneer V represents a solution to the communication problem; launched on March 11, 1960, its solar-powered transmitter was heard for 106 days to a distance of 22.5 million miles from Earth. A flight plan for returning a capsule from orbit had been tested extensively in the Discoverer series charted below.

Cone-like *Vanguard III studied Earth's magnetic field*

← Satellite's path —

Discoverer satellite

Nose-cone separation

Floatable capsule

Air Snatch: C-119 Flying Boxcars equipped with nylon ropes grab the capsule as it plummets to earth

Alaska

Pacific Ocean

Hawaii

The view from 700 miles high—*as an Atlas ICBM began its descent, a 70 mm. camera made this historic picture*

Pioneer V's *solar-cell paddlewheels ran its 5-watt radio*

In one year, *Explorer VII recorded over 1,000 miles of taped data*

297

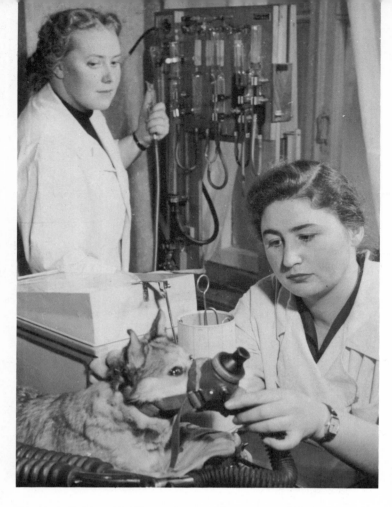

Photographic flashbulbs popped, TV cameras whirred, and the first pairs of Russian and American space travelers made their triumphant returns. With all the ceremony of a state visit, two female dogs named Belka and Strelka and two female monkeys named Able and Baker were hailed for their pioneering roles. The dogs had orbited the Earth 18 times, marking up nearly 500,000 miles in all, before curving back to Earth. The monkeys had soared 300 miles high in ballistic flight over the Atlantic. This was in the classic tradition of research. Whenever possible, animals are used to explore every contingency before man himself ventures forth. But men could only wonder if there was perhaps some

Soviet scientist Ada Kotovskaya and space candidate

Three Russian animal space travelers seem unharmed and unabashed by the press after a 60-mile-high ascent in a rocket

significance to the fact that the first animal pioneers were female.

The two space hazards that man's evolutionary relatives were called upon to explore were weightlessness and radiation. Weightlessness (or zero gravity) is produced in flight when outward momentum nullifies the pull of gravity that man is accustomed to on earth. Pilots who have experienced this free-falling sensation for periods up to 80 seconds during a parabolic airplane maneuver report that it is pleasant. But prolonged zero G may befuddle the sense and upset muscle coordination. Radiation, the second worry, is a phenomenon whose dimensions are only now being plotted.

Mice were particularly well-suited to study both these hazards (see weightless mice at right). Small and sturdy, the mouse has a skin like a bulky overcoat. This permits easy attachment of electrodes for recording a wide variety of physiological effects. They are easy to handle, cheap to feed, and reproduce rapidly—allowing a quick check on radiation's genetic effects. They also neatly fit the snug accommodations of an instrument-jammed nose cone. But, ingenious as the mice experiments are, the greatest interest and attention has focused on the American monkeys and the Russian dogs. A word about their relative merits is necessary. Dogs may be man's best friend, but monkeys are his nearest relatives physically and emotionally. Moreover, monkeys are bright. The Russian space doctors, probably because of the Pavlovian tradition of canine research, have made dogs their favorite experimental tool. But, in their anatomical make-up, and in emotional response, monkeys are akin to man. The two favorite monkeys used in the United States program are the patrician-looking rhesus, a tough, resilient, and ingenious primate weighing in at some seven pounds and the amiable and winsome squirrel monkey. Bright-eyed and long-tailed, the squirrel monkey is the smallest of the primate family.

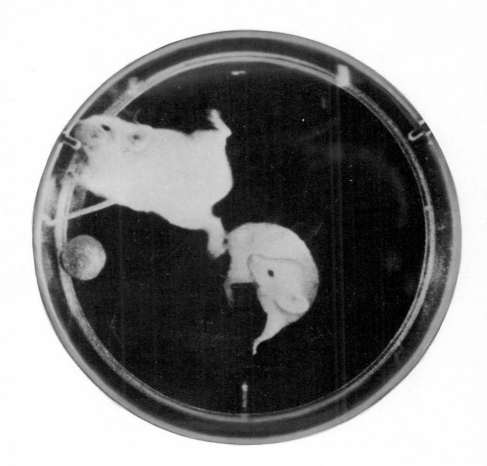

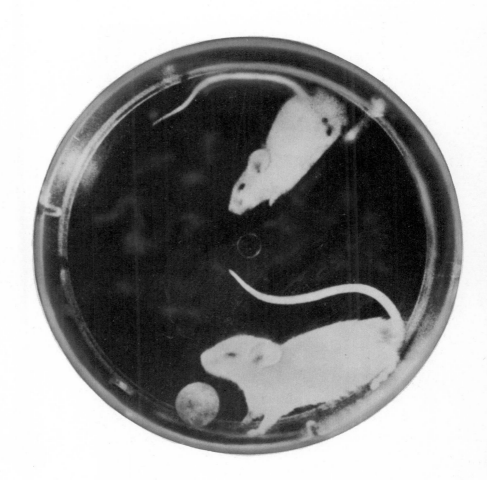

Their names were Able and Baker, impersonal designations taken from the old military phonetic alphabet. But their 300-mile-high voyage over the Atlantic in a Jupiter nose cone launched in May 1959, earned them a personal niche in history. During their flashing, 15-minute flight, the simian pair hit speeds up to 10,000 mph. They were, in fact, models in miniature of the well-equipped spaceman. Both wore molded plastic helmets and were strapped onto a contour couch. And both lay in the prescribed spaceman's position: Knees drawn up and backs turned forward to withstand the severe shocks of atmospheric re-entry at the end of the journey. Baker was primarily a passenger, wired for heartbeat, respiration, and body temperature. Able had a job. Her darkened compartment was equipped with a tiny telegraph key she was to press when a red light flashed once a second. Back on the ground, space medics monitored the reports from the tiny electrodes and concluded that monkeys—and man—could withstand the rigors of space. But the flights left other questions unanswered. What was it really like? The gift of language—the ability to name things—uniquely distinguishes man from the lower primates. Only man could complete the trip log.

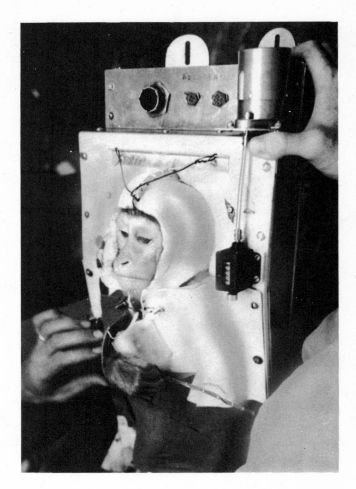

Able in her tailored couch getting a pre-flight check-up

Jupiter nose cone in water, just moments before recovery

View of Able's compartment showing monitoring gear

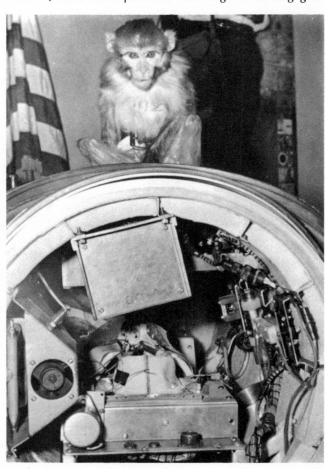

From 500—seven, then one. *American astronauts Carpenter, Cooper, Glenn, Grissom, Schirra, Shepard, Slayton*

Soviet space candidate *Aleksei Grachev is wired with electrodes for a pressure-chamber test*

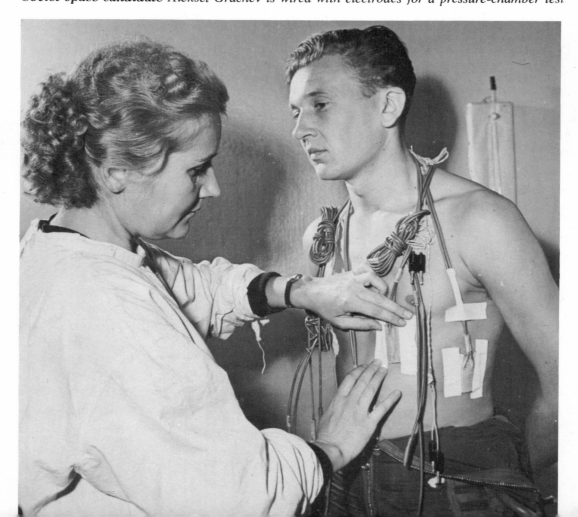

after the years of intensive training, still were impatient for the countdown to quicken, and the incandescent moment out in space

The Anatomy of the Spaceman

Averaging out the vital statistics of the seven men shown across the top of the page, a physical and social portrait emerges which is not much different from that of the suburban homeowner putting up his storm windows across the way. Age: Middle 30s. Weight: 164 pounds. Height: 5 feet 10 inches. Married, with 2.1 children. Salary: $11,331. Recreation: Fishing and hunting. Yet something in their lean, crew-cut good looks showed that they bore a special stamp.

These were the Mercury astronauts—the men chosen to be the first Americans to ride into space. From the original pool of 500 active military test pilots the National Aeronautics and Space Administration in early 1959 culled out the "Superb Seven"—Malcolm Carpenter, Leroy Cooper Jr., John Glenn Jr., Virgil Grissom, Walter Schirra Jr., Alan B. Shepard Jr., and Donald Slayton. Already poised and knowledgeable pilots, the astronauts nevertheless found that they had a rigorous training program facing them. Some of this program, involving physical training and flight proficiency, is shown on the following two pages. But a good part of the astronauts' preparation was not so public and spectacular; there was also, in the words of astronaut Cooper, "the tremendous maze of technical stuff to go through." The brief case, crammed with reports to be read, memoranda to compile, became as much the symbol of Project Mercury as the helmeted spaceman. Inevitably, the astronauts chaffed a bit: "Let's get the tin can up." There was good reason for their concern: In the Soviet Union, another group of test pilots were going through a similar countdown. For, more competitive than ever, the race between the United States and Russia was on. All science was certain to benefit from the findings of the first human space traveler, but the nation that won would score a major political, psychological, and propaganda victory.

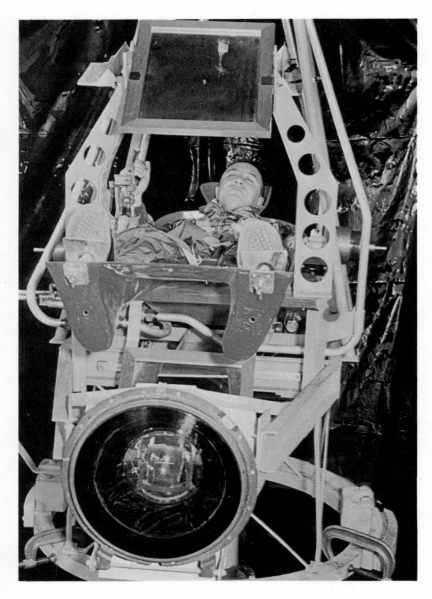

Orbit flight, simulated on this device, teaches control by air jets

Astronaut Cooper spins wildly about in Mercury procedure trainer

Project Mercury's flight plan called for three or four brief, flashing trips from Florida's Cape Canaveral arching 125 miles high over the Atlantic at speeds up to 4,000 mph. Then, satellite flight, the greatest adventure within man's grasp: Three times around the world at 17,000 mph, four hours and 30 minutes in orbit. Finally, splashdown in the Atlantic north of Puerto Rico. For this short but triumphant moment, the astronauts devoted three years of intensive preparations. Over and over again they "flew" the mission in jets and in giant centrifuges—wickedly whirling arms like an amusement park crack-the-whip: First, the awesome pressures of rocket acceleration, what the astronauts called the "eyeballs in" maneuver. Next, the giddy sensation of weightlessness in orbit, then, "eyeballs out"—the deceleration force of slamming back into the atmosphere. The astronauts practiced snaking out of their tight capsule at sea and inflating an emergency raft. There also were desert-survival exercises where each man learned to make his parachute serve as a protective tent. Every eventuality was taken into account. But the astronauts, trained engineers as well as pilots, well knew the first rule of scientific exploration: There is an X factor— the unknown factor in the equation—so expect the unexpected.

Helmeted astronaut pushes away from capsule in sea exercise

Astronaut and golf ball are weightless as jet trainer goes into its roll

The capsule parachute is made into a desert shelter and emergency clothing as part of survival training

W ingless, blunt, squat, the 2,000-pound Mercury capsule designed to take the first American into orbit is shaped like a giant Liberty Bell. Topping it, the escape rocket (to lift the astronaut and capsule free of the booster rocket should any mishap occur during powered flight) adds an incongruous steeple-like tower. All in all, an ungainly looking and unesthetic ship, especially when compared with other manned explorers of the edge of space such as the needle-nosed, sleek North American X-15 rocket plane. But the Mercury is an incredibly complicated and clever machine, webbed with seven miles of wiring, all exposed to save weight. The instrument panel, bearing 112 separate dials, meters, toggles, and buttons, stands a bare 24 inches from the astronaut's nose as he rides his ship into orbit. The capsule carries its own jet power permitting three-way steering while in orbit, oxygen, air-conditioning equipment, cameras, drinking water, the recovery gear (including two sets of parachutes), radios, and a periscope that permits him to view the planet Earth from his contour couch ("Isn't there a nice Earth out tonight?"). But there is little time for philosophic reflections from the astronaut's exalted platform: Over the two-way radio come assignments to test his reactions; he constantly monitors his oxygen reserves, cockpit pressure, and radiation exposure.

Ignition, and the X-15 drops from B-52 and begins arching climb to record-breaking heights of 100 miles

Mercury capsule *undergoes checkout at Cape Canaveral—escape rocket shown at top*

CAPSULE SEPARATED FROM
SUSTAINER ENGINE

ESCAPE UNIT JETTISONED
ROCKET BURNOUT

VENTURE BEYOND

the

ascent

and

return

BOOSTER JETTISONED

CAPSULE LAUNCHING

MAIN CHUTE OPENS
2 MILES

BRAKING CHUTE OPENS
12 MILES

CAPSULE ORIENTATION
TO ORBIT ATTITUDE

CAPSULE PITCH, YAW AND ROLL
CORRECTED BY SMALL JETS

MAINTAIN ORBIT
ATTITUDE

RETRO-ROCKETS FIRE
RE-ENTRY BEGINS

RETRO UNIT
JETTISONED

Overhead the last stars fade in the soft Florida sky. It is dawn—and the waiting is almost over. Inside a van, two men in their mid-thirties lace leather boots over aluminized nylon suits. Outside, a giant searchlight picks up an 85-foot rocket topped by a black-and-white checkered capsule. The United States is ready to commit its first astronaut to flight. One man is designated Primary; the other Alternate, in case any last-minute hitches occur. At T-30, one-half hour before launching, the Primary eases himself into the capsule. Thus, the era of man in space begins for the United States. Ahead looms the incandescent flight. The rocket blasts off, then falls away, its job done. The escape tower also drops off. Automatic jets

THE EARTH

swing the capsule around so that the blunt end faces forward. Inside, some 125 miles above earth, the astronaut himself is riding backward. During the critical moments of re-entry the blunt end takes the 3,000 degree Fahrenheit friction heat. At 70,000 feet and at 10,000 feet, chutes blossom to slow the ship's descent. At splashdown, the ship impacts at 20 mph.

SPOILER OPEN

AERO-DYNAMIC HEATING BEGINS
AS CAPSULE ENTERS ATMOSPHERE

ABLATION OF BLUNT NOSE PROTECTS
CAPSULE BY CARRYING AWAY BULK OF HEAT

Note: In this artist's conception, perspective has been exaggerated, and the complete orbit omitted, in order to depict clearly details of flight.

The old familiar lunar face (left) and the far side as revealed by Lunik III (right) against a close-up of the moon's surface

American version *of manned spaceship on the moon*   **Russian version** *of manned spaceship on the moon*

The Universe at Man's Finger Tips

Russian and American preoccupation with manned flight did not prevent each nation from aiming at other inviting targets. Of these, easily the most tempting was the moon, Earth's original satellite. Bleak, beautiful, enigmatic, the moon has remained the prime symbol of the unattainable throughout the ages. But by 1958 the missilemen had it within their sights. The American rockets fell short or went wide of their lunar target. Then in September 1959 the moon became a symbol of another kind: The Soviet Union hit the moon with a rocket. As it struck, metal tags with the date and the Soviet coat of arms (a hammer and sickle encircled by wreaths) were scattered about. Twenty-two days later, the Russians followed up this feat with another triumph: The rocket Lunik III looped around the lunar far side—the side never seen by man (because as the moon revolves around Earth it also rotates on its axis and keeps the same face toward Earth). There, it took 40 minutes of pictures. The photos, developed aboard Lunik, were then transmitted back to Earth as radio signals and reconstructed. The hidden side of the moon was seen for the first time, courtesy of the Soviet Union. But these were only the opening shots. Simple calculations showed that both nations would have the rocket power to send men to the moon sometime in the '60s.

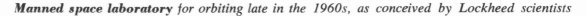

Manned space laboratory *for orbiting late in the 1960s, as conceived by Lockheed scientists*

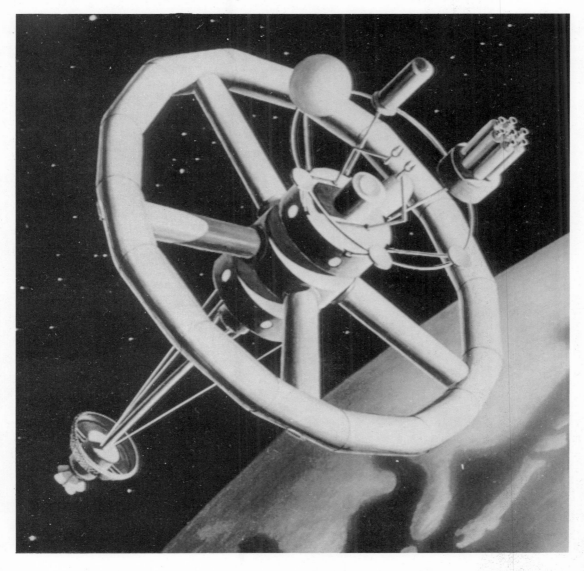

SOLAR FLARE

PHOTOSPHERE

CHROMOSPHERE

SOLAR STORM

SUNSPOTS

PLUTO

URANUS

SATURN

© Copyright C. S. Hammond & Co.

Beyond the moon and satellite flight, man has already raised his sights to other inviting targets. Giant computers have calculated the astronomically precise times and paths for dispatching instrument-carrying rockets to earth's eight sister planets. The trip to Mars, for example, would take 250 days; a Venus voyage, 150 days. What will our robot eyes and ears find there? Mercury, of course, is too close to the sun to offer attractions, but a rocket to the red planet Mars can check on those perplexing canals some observers profess to see. Venus is enticing, since her surface is veiled by dense cloud cover. Beyond are the giant planets: Saturn with its ring of ice particles; giant Jupiter with its 12 moonlets offering a way station and jump-off point; and Pluto, the unknown Tibet of the solar system.

MILKY WAY

NEPTUNE

MARS

EARTH

SUN

VENUS

MERCURY

SAMPLE PROBE TRAJECTORY TO JUPITER

JUPITER

ANDROMEDA GALAXY

GLOBULAR CLUSTERS

THE SOLAR SYSTEM

Well before the first astronauts embarked on their great human adventure, another group of young Americans began an even more incredible quest: An attempt to make contact with civilizations that astronomers calculate are reasonably certain to exist elsewhere in the universe. The instrument of this attempt was the radio telescope, the giant electronic ears which can span galactic distances and monitor radiations given off by large star populations 38 billion light years away. The search began in 1960, at the beginning of the new decade, in a secluded West Virginia valley where the United States National Radio Astronomy Observatory has its big dishes (see right). The first search proved fruitless. But the observatory persevered. As its director, Otto Struve, remarked: "Unless we try, we will never know."

England's Jodrell Bank radiotelescope—an ear tuned to space

Powerful, subtle scopes are steered precisely

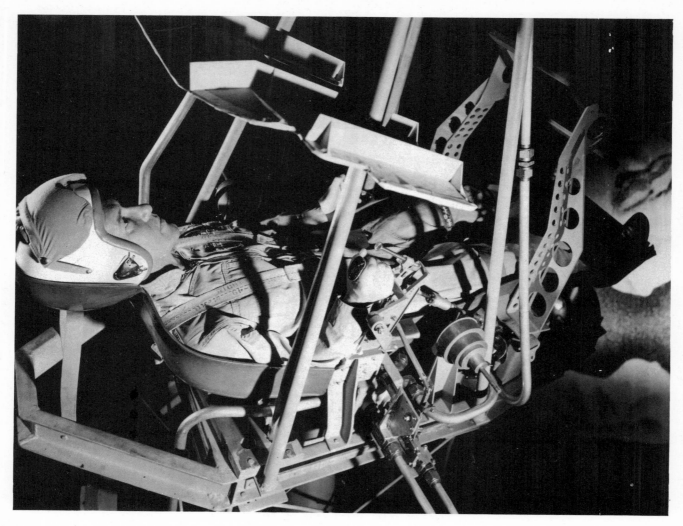

Whether the first space explorer was to be an American astronaut (above) or a Russian cosmonaut (below), all mankind would ride with him

Tricked by his eyes, imprisoned by gravity, fallible, frail, vain, egocentric, man has taken centuries to realize the truths about his place in the universe: He is only one of a thousand forms of life on the crust of a minor planet of a second-rate star near the edge of a local galaxy called the Milky Way; there are other intelligent players on the stage of the universe; this planet Earth, its race of humans, may not be the ultimate expression of nature. But in these truths there is another and deeper truth. In the words of the French philosopher Montesquieu: "We have come a long way —for men." Indeed, as the first Earth pioneers set forth on their journey into the alien cosmos, all men can look back and take pride in how far they have come.

Photographic and Painting Credits

The World of Imperialism

Page 6: British Information Services. **Pages 8-9:** Culver Pictures, Inc. **Page 8:** Culver Pictures, Inc. **Page 9:** *Above;* Gernsheim Collection. *Below;* Bettmann Archive. **Page 10:** *Above;* Disraeli, Sir J.E. Millais, National Portrait Gallery, London. *Below;* Illustrated London News. **Page 11:** *Above, Below Left and Right;* Bettmann Archive. **Page 14:** *Above;* Culver Pictures, Inc. *Below Left;* Gene Badger, Rapho Guillumette. *Below Left Center;* British Information Services. *Below Right Center;* Brown Brothers. *Below Right;* United Nations. **Page 15:** *Above;* Culver Pictures, Inc. *Below Left;* British Information Services. *Below Center;* United Nations. *Below Right;* Gullers, Rapho Guillumette. **Page 17:** *Above and Below;* Bettmann Archive. **Page 18:** Keystone. **Page 19:** *Above;* Bettmann Archive. **Page 20:** *Above;* George V, Sir Oswald Birley, National Portrait Gallery, London. *Below;* John Cowan. **Page 21:** Brown Brothers. **Page 22:** *Above;* Bismarck Before Paris, Louis Braun, Courtesy of Franz Hanfstaengl, Munich. *Below;* Culver Pictures, Inc. **Pages 24-25:** Bivouac Devant le Bourget, Alphonse de Neuville, Musée de Dijon. **Page 26:** Brown Brothers. **Page 27:** *Above;* Culver Pictures, Inc. *Below;* Ullstein, Bonn. **Page 30:** *Above;* U.S. Navy. *Center;* Brown Brothers. **Page 31:** *Above;* Culver Pictures, Inc. *Below Left and Right;* Bettmann Archive. **Page 32:** *Above;* Le Bal á Bougival, Pierre Auguste Renoir, Museum of Fine Arts, Boston. *Below;* Jane Avril Dansant, Henri de Toulouse-Lautrec, Musée du Louvre, Galerie du Jeu de Paume, Photographie Giraudon. **Page 33:** *Above;* Boulevard des Italiens, Morning, Sunlight, Camille Pissarro, Chester Dale Collection, National Gallery of Art, Washington, D.C. *Below;* La Loge, Pierre Auguste Renoir, Courtauld Collection, Courtauld Institute Galleries. **Page 34:** *Left;* Culver Pictures, Inc. *Right;* UPI. **Page 35:** *Above;* Bettmann Archive. **Page 36:** Bataille de la Mouzaïa, Joseph Bellangé, Musée Condé, Chantilly, Photographie Giraudon. **Page 38:** European. **Page 39:** *Above;* Culver Pictures, Inc. *Below Left, Center and Right;* Illustrirte Zeitung. **Pages 40-41:** Hofball, Wilhelm Gause, Historical Museum of the City of Vienna. **Page 42:** *Above;* Leaving the Imperial Palace, Alexander Pock, Picture Archives, Austrian National Library. *Below;* Stairway in Upper Belvedere, Rudolf von Alt, Graphische Sammlung Albertina, Vienna. **Page 43:** *Below;* Café Griensteidl, Rudolf Voelkel, Historical Museum of the City of Vienna. **Page 44:** Morning Training in the Spanish Court Riding School, Julius von Blaas, Spanish Riding Academy, Vienna. **Page 45:** Viennese Philharmonic Orchestra, August Mandlick, Picture Archives, Austrian National Library. **Page 46:** *Above;* Picture Archives, Austrian National Library. *Below;* Emperor Franz Josef I, Picture Archives, Austrian National Library. **Page 47:** Culver Pictures, Inc. **Page 50:** *Above;* Police Protecting Parliament, Friedrich Kaskeline, Picture Archives, Austrian National Library. *Below;* Clash on the Viennese Ringstrasse, Wilhelm Gause, Picture Archives, Austrian National Library. **Page 51:** *Above;* Interior of Croatian Farmer's House, Franz Schlegel, Picture Archives, Austrian National Library. *Below;* Picture Archives, Austrian National Library. **Page 52:** *Above;* European. *Below;* Assassination of Archduke Franz Ferdinand, Felix Schwarmstadt, Picture Archives, Austrian National Library. **Page 53:** *Above;* Kaiser-Manöver, Alexander Pock, Picture Archives, Austrian National Library. *Below;* Franz Josef Mourning, Felix Schwarmstadt, Picture Archives, Austrian National Library. **Pages 54-55:** Return From Market, Joseph Chelmonski, Present Owner Unknown. **Page 56:** *Above;* Les Solennités du Saint Couronnement, Rare Book Division, New York Public Library. *Below;* Museum of Russian Culture, Inc., San Francisco. **Page 57:** *Above Left and Right;* Museum of Russian Culture, Inc., San Francisco. *Below;* Les Solennités du Saint Couronnement, Rare Book Division, New York Public Library. **Pages 58-59:** UPI. **Page 59:** Culver Pictures, Inc. **Page 62:** Brown Brothers. **Page 63:** UPI. **Page 64:** Emperor Mutsuhito, Haisui Takagi, Meiji Museum, Tokyo. **Page 68:** *Above Left;* Opening Fire of Russo-Japan Sea Battle, Fusetsu Nakamura, Meiji Museum, Tokyo. *Above Right;* Triumphant Review of the Imperial Fleet, Shotaro Tojo, Meiji Museum, Tokyo. *Below;* Theodore Roosevelt, John Singer Sargent, White House, Washington, D.C. **Page 69:** Culver Pictures, Inc. **Page 70:** *Above and Below;* Brown Brothers. **Page 71:** European. **Page 74:** *Above;* European. *Below;* British Information Services. **Page 75:** *Above and Below;* Culver Pictures, Inc. **Page 76:** U.S.S.R. Magazine, Sovfoto. **Page 77:** U.S.S.R. Magazine, Sovfoto. **Page 78:** Rex Features, London. **Page 79:** Exécution, S. Sarmat, Histoire des Soviéts.

The World of Idealism and Upheaval

Page 82: Charles Phelps Cushing. **Pages 84-85:** Armistice Night, George Luks, Anonymous Gift, Whitney Museum of American Art, New York. **Page 86:** *Above Left;* UPI. *Above Right;* Wide World. *Below;* Culver Pictures, Inc. **Page 87:** *Above and Below;* European. **Page 88:** L'Illustration. **Page 89:** Signing of the Versailles Peace Treaty, John C. Johansen, National Collection of Fine Arts, Smithsonian Institution. **Page 90:** *Above;* Underwood and Underwood. *Below;* Bettmann Archive. **Page 91:** *Above;* UPI. *Below;* Bettmann Archive. **Page 94:** *Above Left and Right;* Brown Brothers. *Below;* Culver Pictures, Inc. **Page 95:** *Above Left;* UPI. *Above Right;* European. *Below Left;* Culver Pictures, Inc. *Below Right;* Wide World. **Page 98:** *Above and Below;* UPI. **Page 99:** *Above;* Culver Pictures, Inc. *Below;* European. **Page 100:** The Passion of Sacco and Vanzetti, Ben Shahn, Gift of Edith and Milton Lowenthal in Memory of Juliana Force, Whitney Museum of American Art, New York. **Page 101:** *Above;* Texas Guinan and Her Gang, Reginald Marsh, Edward W. Root Bequest, Munson-Williams-Proctor Institute. *Below;* McSorley's Bar, Saturday Night, John Sloan, Joseph H. Hirshhorn Collection. **Page 102:** *Above Left;* Brown Brothers. *Above Right;* European. *Below;* Brown Brothers. **Page 103:** *Above;* Bettmann Archive. *Below Left;* UPI. *Below Right;* Brown Brothers. **Page 106:** *Above Center, Right, and Below;* Wide World. **Page 107:** *Above Left;* Wide World. *Above Right;* European. *Below;* Romer Historic Files. **Page 108:** Brown Brothers. **Page 110:** *Above;* UPI. *Below;* Wide World. **Page 111:** The Unemployed, Kaethe Kollwitz, Galerie St. Etienne, New York. **Page 112:** *Above;* Vienna Is Dying! Save Its Children!, Kaethe Kollwitz, Galerie St. Etienne, New York. *Below;* UPI. **Page 113:** *Above;* Missouri Historical Society. *Below Left;* Brown Brothers. *Below Right;* UPI. **Page 114:** *Above;* Charles Phelps Cushing. *Below;* UPI. **Page 115:** *Above;* UPI. *Center;* Brown Brothers. **Pages 116-117:** American Farm, Joe Jones, Whitney Museum of American Art, New York. **Page 118:** *Above;* UPI. *Below;* European. **Page 119:** *Below;* European. **Page 121:** *Above;* Employment Agency, Isaac Soyer, Whitney Museum of American Art, New York. *Below;* Charles Phelps Cushing.

The World of Dictators

Page 122: Wide World. **Page 126:** *Above Left;* UPI. *Above Right;* European. **Page 127:** *Left;* European. *Above and Center Right;* Birnback. *Below Right;* Culver Pictures, Inc. **Page 129:** 1932, Jack Levine, Mr. and Mrs. Dalton Trumbo. **Page 130:** *Above;* Wide World. *Below;* European. **Page 131:** *Above;* Wide World. *Below;* UPI. **Page 134:** UPI. **Page 137:** *Above;* European. *Below;* The Lion of Judah, Arthur Szyk. **Page 138:** *Above;* European. *Below;* Combine. **Page**

139: European. **Page 140:** Historia de la Cruzada Española. **Page 141:** Guernica, Pablo Picasso, Collection, Museum of Modern Art, New York. **Page 142:** *Above Left*; Sovfoto. *Above Right and Below*; European. **Page 143:** *Above*; European. *Below Left and Right*; Wide World. **Pages 144-145:** Serge Korolkoff. **Page 146:** *Above*; Wide World. *Below*; UPI. **Page 147:** *Above and Below Left*; European. *Below Right*; UPI. **Page 148:** *Left*; UPI. *Right*; Pravda. **Page 150:** *Left*; Wide World. *Right*; Pictorial Parade. **Page 151:** *Above and Below*; Culver Pictures, Inc. **Page 152:** Through the Mill, Philip Evergood, Whitney Museum of American Art, New York. **Page 153:** American Tragedy, Philip Evergood, Armand G. Erpf Collection. **Page 154:** *Above*; UPI. *Below*; Culver Pictures, Inc. **Page 155:** *Above*; Brown Brothers. *Below*; UPI. **Pages 156-157:** Charles Phelps Cushing. **Page 158:** *Above and Below*; Wide World. **Page 159:** *Above Left and Right*; European. *Below Left*; UPI. *Below Right*; European. **Page 160:** *Above*; Twentieth Century Fox. *Below*; Universal Pictures. **Page 161:** *Above and Below*; Metro Goldwyn Mayer. **Page 162:** *Above and Below*; Wide World. **Page 163:** *Above*; UPI. *Below Left*; Wide World. *Below Right*; UPI. **Page 164:** *Above Left*; UPI. *Above Right and Below*; Brown Brothers. **Page 165:** Raphael Tuck and Sons, Ltd. **Page 166:** *Above*; Fox Photos, London. *Below*; Wide World. **Page 167:** *Above Left*; Imperial War Museum, London. *Center Left*; European. *Below Left*; Wide World. *Right*; Radio Times Hulton Picture Library, London. **Page 169:** Deauville Racetrack, Raoul Dufy, Gift of Mrs. Gerald Parker and Mr. Earle Grant in Memory of Mrs. T.J. Flannelly, Nelson Gallery—Atkins Museum. **Page 170:** *Above*; Viollet. *Below*; European. **Page 171:** *Above Left and Right*; UPI. *Below*; Wide World. **Page 173:** Newsweek—Ed Wergeles. **Page 174:** *Above*; Picture Archives, Austrian National Library. *Below Left*; Wide World. *Below Right*; Brown Brothers. **Page 175:** *Above*; UPI. *Below Left*; Wide World. *Below Right*; European. **Page 177:** History of the Second World War in Cartoons, Ignacio Carral y de Icaza, Antonio Arias Bernal, Mexico. **Page 178:** *Above*; Birnback. *Below*; Wide World. **Page 180:** Wide World. **Page 181:** Fox Photos, London. **Page 182:** *Above and Below*; Wide World. **Page 183:** *Above*; Combine. *Below*; UPI. **Page 184:** *Above and Below*; Julien Bryan, IFF. **Page 185:** Julien Bryan, IFF. **Page 186:** *Above and Below Left*; Wide World. *Below Right*; Culver Pictures, Inc. **Page 187:** *Above*; Withdrawal from Dunkirk, Charles Cundall, Imperial War Museum, London. *Below*; Wide World. **Pages 188-189:** Griffiths Bailey Coale, U.S. Navy. **Page 188:** Imperial War Museum, London. **Page 189:** U.S. Navy. **Page 190:** *Above*; Culver Pictures, Inc. *Below*; New York Times. **Page 191:** UPI. **Page 192:** Griffiths Bailey Coale, U.S. Navy. **Page 193:** *Above*; U.S. Air Force. *Below*; U.S. Marine Corps. **Page 194:** *Above*; Wide World. *Below Left*; U.S. Army. *Below Right*; European. **Page 195:** *Above Left*; Wide World. *Center Left and Above Right*; UPI. *Below*; Paris Match. **Page 196:** *Above*; U.S. Army. *Below*; Thomas Hollyman, Photo Researchers. **Page 197:** *Above*; Under the Mushroom at Hiroshima, R. Munsell Chambers, U.S. Air Force. *Below*; The Rising Sun, R. Munsell Chambers, U.S. Air Force.

The World of Nationalism

Page 198: Newsweek—Tony Rollo. **Pages 202-203:** European. **Page 204:** *Below*; UPI. **Page 205:** *Above and Below*; U.S. Army. **Page 206:** *Above*; UPI. *Below*; Wide World. **Page 207:** *Above*; Brown Brothers. *Below*; Wide World. **Pages 210-211:** Wide World. **Page 210:** *Above and Below*; Charles Phelps Cushing. **Page 211:** Wide World. **Page 214:** *Above*; Wide World. *Below*; UPI. **Page 215:** *Left*; Wide World. *Right*; Harvard University Archives. **Page 216:** *Left and Right*; Wide World. **Page 217:** *Left*; Wide World. *Right*; UPI. **Page 218:** *Above*; UPI. *Below*; Wide World. **Page 219:** *Above Left and Right*; UPI. *Center*; Wide World. *Below*; European. **Page 222:** European. **Page 223:** *Above*; UPI. *Below*; European. **Page 226:** European. **Page 227:** *Above*; Sovfoto. *Center and Below*; UPI. **Page 228:** *Above and Below*; Harrison Forman. **Page 229:** Harrison Forman. **Page 230:** *Above*; UPI. *Below Left*; European. *Below Right*; Wide World. **Page 231:** Newsweek—Tony Rollo. **Pages 232-233:** Bill Stapleton. **Page 232:** Bill Stapleton. **Page 233:** European. **Page 234:** *Above and Below*; UPI. **Page 235:** UPI. **Page 236:** Harrison Forman. **Page 237:** *Above and Below*; Pictorial Parade. **Page 238:** Pictorial Parade. **Page 239:** *Above*; Eastfoto. *Below*; Sovfoto. **Page 241:** U.S. Atomic Energy Commission. **Page 242:** *Above*; London Daily Express. *Center*; Birnback. **Page 243:** *Above*; Henry Grossman. *Below*; Wide World. **Pages 244-245:** Illingworth, London Daily Mail. **Page 244:** *Above*; Pictorial Parade. *Above Center*; Wide World. *Below Center and Below*; UPI. **Page 245:** Wide World. **Page 246:** *Above*; London Daily Express. *Below Left*; UPI. *Below Right*; U.S. Navy. **Page 247:** Newsweek—Lionel Durand. **Page 248:** Newsweek—Ed Wergeles. **Page 249:** *Above*; British Information Services. *Below*; Eastfoto. **Page 250:** *Above*; Punch, Ben Roth. *Below*; Eastfoto. **Page 251:** Henri Cartier-Bresson, Magnum. **Pages 254-255:** UPI. **Page 254:** Newsweek—Vytas Valaitis. **Page 255:** UPI. **Page 256:** *Above*; UPI. *Below*; Wide World. **Page 258:** *Above and Below*; Wide World. **Page 259:** *Above*; Magnum. *Below*; UPI. **Page 262:** *Above*; Throckmorton, Monkmeyer. *Below*; United Nations. **Page 263:** *Above, Below Left and Right*; Newsweek—Vytas Valaitis. **Page 264:** Newsweek—Vytas Valaitis. **Pages 264-265:** Newsweek—Tony Rollo.

The World of Space

Page 266: Newsweek—Bob Lavin. **Pages 268-269:** Lick Observatory, University of California. **Pages 270-271:** Ornithopter, Leonardo da Vinci, IBM Corporation. **Page 270:** *Above*; Flight of Icarus, Mythology in Prints, Lester M. Prindle. *Below*; Larousse Encyclopedia of Astronomy, Prometheus Press. **Page 271:** *Above*; Bella C. Landauer Collection. *Below*; Culver Pictures, Inc. **Page 272:** *Above*; Bettmann Archive. *Below*; Brown Brothers. **Pages 272-273:** Bettmann Archive. **Page 273:** Charles Phelps Cushing. **Page 274:** *Above*; Hayden Planetarium. *Below Left and Right*; Brown Brothers. **Page 275:** *Above*; Dr. Leon L. Watters. *Below*; Wide World. **Page 276:** Wilson Hole Studios. **Page 277:** Wilson Hole Studios. **Page 278:** *Above*; Wide World. *Below*; California Institute of Technology. **Page 279:** *Above*; California Institute of Technology. *Below*; Mount Wilson and Palomar Observatories. **Page 280:** Paul Melone. **Page 281:** James MacDonald, Rockets and Jets, Copyright Herbert S. Zim, 1945, Permission of Harcourt, Brace & World, Inc. **Page 282:** Wide World. **Page 283:** Sovfoto. **Page 284:** *Above*; Charles H. Houbell, Thompson Ramo Wooldridge, Inc. *Below*; U.S. Army, **Page 285:** *Above*; U.S. Army. *Below*; UPI. **Page 286:** *Left*; General Dynamics Corporation. *Center and Right*; UPI. **Page 287:** *Above*; Keystone. *Below*; Wide World. **Page 288:** Newsweek. **Pages 288-289:** Smithsonian Astrophysical Observatory. **Page 290:** *Above, Below Left and Right*; Sovfoto. **Page 291:** *Above*; California Institute of Technology. *Below*; UPI. **Page 294:** *Above Left*; U.S. Navy. *Center Left*; NASA. *Below Left*; U.S. Army. *Right*; Wide World. **Page 295:** *Above*; Wide World. *Below*; Newsweek—Walter Bensi. **Page 296:** *Above*; NASA. *Below*; Newsweek—D.W. Van Dyke. **Page 297:** *Above*; U.S. Air Force. *Below Left*; NASA. *Below Right*; U.S. Air Force. **Page 298:** *Above and Below*; Sovfoto. **Page 299:** *Above and Below*; Wide World. **Page 300:** *Above*; Brown Brothers. *Below Left*; UPI. *Below Right*; Wide World. **Page 301:** NASA. **Pages 302-303:** McDonnell Aircraft Corporation. **Page 302:** Sovfoto. **Page 304:** *Above and Below*; NASA. **Page 305:** *Above, Below Left and Right*; NASA. **Page 306:** North American Aviation, Inc. **Page 307:** NASA. **Page 310:** *Above*; Mount Wilson and Palomar Observatories. *Above Left*; Lick Observatory, University of California. *Above Right*; Wide World. *Below Right*; UPI. **Page 311:** Wide World. **Page 314:** *Left*; Neil Libbert, London Observer. *Right*; London Daily Express. **Page 315:** U.S. Navy. **Page 316:** *Above*; NASA. *Below*; UPI. **Page 317:** Ralph Iligan, U.S. Air Force.